POSTCONVICTION FORMS

for the

FLORIDA PRISONER

Loren Rhoton

Postconviction Forms for the Florida Prisoner
A publication of Loren Rhoton, P.A.

ISBN: 978-0-9822800-8-9

DISCLAIMER

This book is not intended to provide legal advice or to take the place of legal counsel. This book should be used as an educational and reference source for persons interested in pursuing postconviction remedies. Readers are advised to consult with an attorney if they intend to pursue a postconviction action. The information provided in this book is general in nature and may not be applicable to any given legal case. This publication is not a substitute for the advice of an attorney.

Contact Loren Rhoton, P.A., at:
412 E. Madison Street
Suite 1111
Tampa, Florida 33602
lorenrhoton@rhotonpostconviction.com
rhotonpostconviction.com

CONTENTS

Introduction and a Note on Use of Forms 1
Form 1 – Notice of Appeal 2
Form 2 – Motion to Declare Appellant Indigent with Affidavit of Insolvency 3
Form 3 – Directions to Clerk 6
Form 4 – Designation to Court Reporter 7
Form 5 – Motion to Reduce/Mitigate Sentence 9
Form 6 – Motion for Extension of Time to File Brief 11
Form 7 – Notice of Supplemental Authority 12
Form 8 – Motion to Supplement The Record on Appeal 13
Form 9 – Motion to Exceed Page Limit in Brief 15
Form 10 – Voluntary Dismissal of Appeal 17
Form 11 – Initial Appellate Brief 18
Form 12 – Request for Oral Argument 22
Form 13 – Motion for Rehearing 23
Form 14 – Motion for Written Opinion 25
Form 15 – Motion for Certification 27
Form 16 – Notice to Invoke Discretionary Jurisdiction of Florida Supreme Court 28
Form 17 – Rule 3.850 Motion for Postconviction Relief and Supporting Memorandum 29
Form 18 – Motion to File Belated 3.850 Motion 35
Form 19 – Motion to Limit Scope of Use of Testimony and Evidence Proffered at Evidentiary Hearing 39

Form 20 – Motion for Court to Rule on Movant's Motion for Postconviction Relief 42
Form 21 – Petition for Writ of Mandamus 44
Form 22 – Motion for Permission to Conduct Limited Discovery on Motion for Postconviction Relief 47
Form 23 – Motion to Correct Illegal Sentence 49
Form 24 – Motion to Disqualify Judge 50
Form 25 – Petition for Writ of Prohibition 53
Form 26 – Public Records Request 56
Appendix A – Title 28 U.S.C. §2254 Petition for Writ of Habeas Corpus Form 57
Appendix B - Title 28 U.S.C. §2255 Motion to Vacate, Set Aside, or Correct a Sentence by a Person in Federal Custody Form 74
Appendix C – Selected Florida Rules of Criminal Procedure 88
Appendix D – Selected Rules of Appellate Procedure 116
Appendix E – Jurisdiction of Florida Courts 132
About The Author 135

INTRODUCTION and a NOTE on USE of FORMS

This formbook is geared toward indigent Florida prisoners who find themselves in the position of having to seek postconviction relief without the help of an attorney. The formbook is essentially a companion to my legal self-help book *Postconviction Relief for the Florida Prisoner*. The forms are for the most common types of pleadings that will need to be filed in Florida postconviction cases and give examples of how such motions should be prepared. However, the motions do not cover every possible argument or factual scenario that may need to be presented. Where a form does not address specific issues, it should be altered to include any necessary information that is pertinent to a particular case.

The forms provided in this book are intended to satisfy pleading requirements under the Florida rules and statutes. But, rules of procedure and statutes are regularly amended, so it is advisable when relying on the forms to also check applicable statutes and rules for any pleading requirements that may have changed. The forms in this book are merely examples of how certain motions should look. They are a good starting point in drafting postconviction motions. But, they should not be relied upon exclusively for drafting important pleadings.

Finally, the appendix includes copies of applicable statutes and other helpful material. Included in the appendix are the approved forms, with instructions, for federal habeas corpus petitions for collateral attacks on both state and federal convictions.

FORM 1 – NOTICE OF APPEAL

IN THE CIRCUIT COURT OF THE ________ JUDICIAL CIRCUIT,
IN AND FOR ____________ COUNTY, FLORIDA

[***DEFENDANT***],

v. Case No.:______________

STATE OF FLORIDA,
______________________/

NOTICE OF APPEAL OF ORDER

NOTICE IS GIVEN that [***DEFENDANT***], the defendant herein, seeks to invoke the jurisdiction of the ____ District Court of Appeal for review of the [***date***], final judgment of this Court. The nature of the order appealed is __________.

I HEREBY CERTIFY that a true copy of the foregoing has been furnished by regular U.S. Mail, this [***date***], to the Office of the State Attorney, [***address***]; and, the Office of the Attorney General, [***address***].

_(signature line)__________
[***Name, DC#, Address***]

FORM 2 – MOTION TO DECLARE APPELLANT INDIGENT WITH AFFIDAVIT OF INSOLVENCY

IN THE CIRCUIT COURT OF THE ________ JUDICIAL CIRCUIT,
IN AND FOR ____________ COUNTY, FLORIDA

[***DEFENDANT***],

v. Case No.:_____________

STATE OF FLORIDA,
____________________/

MOTION TO DECLARE DEFENDANT
INDIGENT FOR PURPOSES OF APPEAL

COMES NOW [***DEFENDANT***] and requests that this Honorable Court find the Defendant to be indigent for the purpose of appeal, and states:

1. In the instant case this Honorable Court held an evidentiary hearing on [***DEFENDANT's***] Florida Rule of Criminal Procedure 3.850 Motion for Post Conviction Relief.

2. On [***date***] this Court entered an Order denying [***DEFENDANT's***] 3.850 Motion. [***DEFENDANT***] filed a timely notice of appeal of the denial of his 3.850.

3. [***DEFENDANT***] is insolvent and does not have the funds to pay for an attorney or the record on appeal in the instant case. See Exhibit A, Affidavit of Insolvency.

WHEREFORE, [***DEFENDANT***] respectfully requests that this Court grant this motion and adjudge [***DEFENDANT***] indigent for the purposes of his appeal in the instant case.

_(signature line)_______________
[***Name, DC#, Address***]

CERTIFICATE OF SERVICE

I HEREBY CERTIFY that a true copy of the foregoing has been furnished by regular U.S. Mail, this [***date***], to the Office of the State Attorney, [***State Attorney's address***].

_(signature line)________________
[***Name***]

****

Attach Affidavit of Insolvency to Motion

****

IN THE CIRCUIT COURT OF THE _________ JUDICIAL CIRCUIT,
IN AND FOR ____________ COUNTY, FLORIDA

[***DEFENDANT***],

v. Case No.:______________

STATE OF FLORIDA,
______________________/

AFFIDAVIT OF INDIGENCY

BEFORE ME, the undersigned authority personally appeared Affiant, [***DEFENDANT***], who being first duly sworn, deposes and says that:

1. I am over eighteen years of age and have knowledge as to the facts set forth herein.

2. I am the defendant in the above styled cause.

3. I am appealing an order issued by this court denying my Florida Rule of Criminal Procedure 3.850 Motion for Post Conviction Relief.

4. I am insolvent at this time.

5. I am currently incarcerated and have no funds with which I can pay the costs of any judicial proceedings in this cause, including expenses for the preparation of the record on appeal.

6. I have not divested myself of any property, either personal or real in order to take advantage of this oath.

FURTHER AFFIANT SAYETH NOT.

I, [***DEFENDANT***], have read the foregoing and state that the information contained therein is true and correct and of my own personal knowledge.

_(signature line)_______________
[***Name, DC#, Address***]

STATE OF FLORIDA
COUNTY OF _____________

Subscribed and sworn to me on this ___ day of _______, 20__, by [***DEFENDANT***], who is personally known to me or who provided for identification the following:________________.

My Commission Expires:

____

____
Printed Notary Name

____
Signature of Acknowledger
Typed, Printed or Stamped

FORM 3 – DIRECTIONS TO CLERK

IN THE CIRCUIT COURT OF THE ________ JUDICIAL CIRCUIT,
IN AND FOR ___________ COUNTY, FLORIDA

[***DEFENDANT***],

v. Case No.:____________

STATE OF FLORIDA.
____________________/

DIRECTIONS TO CLERK

[***DEFENDANT***] directs the Clerk of the ____ Judicial Circuit Court, in and for ________ County, Florida, to include in the record on appeal, all items contemplated in Rule 9.141(b)* Florida Rules of Appellate Procedure, together with:

1. Any and all exhibits entered into evidence at the [***date***], evidentiary hearing held on [***DEFENDANT's***] Rule 3.850 motion.

2. [***List any other documents, pleadings, et cetera, that are necessary for inclusion in the record on appeal***].

I HEREBY CERTIFY that a true copy of the foregoing has been furnished by regular U.S. Mail, this [***date***], to the Office of the State Attorney, [***State Attorney's address***].

_(signature line)_______________
[***Name, DC#, Address***]

***Publisher's note**: If pursuing direct appeal, request all matters provided for in Rule 9.140(b)(2)(B) Florida Rules of Appellate Procedure.

FORM 4 – DESIGNATION TO COURT REPORTER

IN THE CIRCUIT COURT OF THE ________ JUDICIAL CIRCUIT,
IN AND FOR ___________ COUNTY, FLORIDA

[***DEFENDANT***],

v. Case No.:_____________

STATE OF FLORIDA.
___________________/

DESIGNATION TO REPORTER AND REPORTER'S ACKNOWLEDGMENT
I. DESIGNATION

THE DEFENDANT hereby files this Designation to Reporter and directs [***Court Reporter's name***], to transcribe an original and two copies of the proceedings in the above-captioned matter to be used in this appeal:

1. The proceedings from the following dates:
a. [***Date***].
b. [***Date***].

2. The approved court reporter, civil court reporter, or approved transcriptionist is directed to file the original with the clerk of the lower tribunal and to serve one copy on each of the following:
a. [***DEFENDANT***].
b. The Office of the Attorney General at [***email service address***].

I, [***DEFENDANT***], certify that I have contacted the court reporter, and satisfactory arrangements have been made for the preparation of the transcript.

_(signature line)_______________
[***Name, DC#, Address***]

II.

1. The foregoing designation was served and received on [***date***].

2. Satisfactory arrangements have been made for the payment of the transcript cost. These financial arrangements were completed on [***date***].

3. Number of trial or hearing dates: ___

4. Estimated number of transcript pages: ___

5. The transcript will be available within twenty days of service of the foregoing designation and will be filed on or before [***date***].

OR

For the following reason(s) the court reporter requests an extension of time of ____ days for preparation of the transcript(s) that will be filed on or before [***date***].

6. Completion and filing of this acknowledgment by the court reporter constitutes submission to the jurisdiction of the court for all purposes in connection with these appellate proceedings.

7. The undersigned court reporter certifies that the foregoing is true and correct and that and that a copy has been furnished by email to each of the parties or their counsel.

____

[***Court reporter name, address, phone number, and email address***]

FORM 5 – MOTION TO REDUCE/MITIGATE SENTENCE

IN THE CIRCUIT COURT OF THE ________ JUDICIAL CIRCUIT,
IN AND FOR ____________ COUNTY, FLORIDA

[***DEFENDANT***],

v. Case No.:_____________

STATE OF FLORIDA.
______________________/

RULE 3.800(c) MOTION TO REDUCE SENTENCE

[***DEFENDANT***], pursuant to Florida Rule of Criminal Procedure 3.800(c), hereby moves this Honorable Court to mitigate his sentence, and states:

1. On [***date***], [***DEFENDANT***] was charged by [***information <u>or</u> indictment***] with: [***specify charges***].

2. On [***date***], [***DEFENDANT***] was convicted of ______________.

3. On [***date***], this Honorable Court sentenced [***DEFENDANT***] as follows: _________________.

4. [***DEFENDANT***] appealed the judgment and sentence to the ___ District Court of Appeal. His judgment and sentence was affirmed, *per curiam*, on [***date***]. The Mandate was issued on [***date***].

5. It is respectfully submitted that there are several factors that this Court can take into account and consider in reducing [***DEFENDANT's***] currently imposed sentence, to wit: [***specify mitigating factors***].

6. It is respectfully submitted that [***DEFENDANT's***] behavior since the time he was charged in the instant case, along with the mitigation evidence which has been supplied to this Honorable Court, would justify a sentence reduction at this time.

WHEREFORE, [***DEFENDANT***] respectfully requests that this Honorable Court grant this motion and impose a reduced sentence.

_(signature line)_______________
[***Name, DC#, Address***]

CERTIFICATE OF SERVICE

I HEREBY CERTIFY that a true copy of the foregoing has been furnished by regular U.S. Mail, this [***date***], to the Office of the State Attorney, [***State Attorney's address***].

_(signature line)________________
[***Name***]

FORM 6 – MOTION FOR EXTENSION OF TIME TO FILE BRIEF

IN THE DISTRICT COURT OF APPEAL,
__________ DISTRICT

[***APPELLANT***],
Appellant,
v. Case No.:____________

STATE OF FLORIDA,
Appellee.
____________________/

MOTION FOR EXTENSION OF TIME
TO FILE INITIAL BRIEF

[***APPELLANT***] requests that this Court grant a thirty day extension of time for the Appellant to file his initial brief and states:

1. [***APPELLANT's***] appeal of the denial of his Rule 3.850 motion for postconviction relief is currently pending in the above-captioned case.

2. The Appellant's initial brief is due before this Honorable Court on [***date***].

3. [***APPELLANT***] is unable to timely file his initial brief because [***give reasons for inability to timely file brief***].

4. The instant motion is made in good faith and not for the purposes of delay.

WHEREFORE, the Appellant prays that this Court enter an Order granting the Appellant a thirty-day extension of time to file his initial brief.

_(signature line)_______________
[***Name, DC#, Address***]

CERTIFICATE OF SERVICE

I HEREBY CERTIFY that a true copy of the foregoing has been furnished by regular U.S. Mail, this [***date***], to the Office of the Attorney General, [***Attorney General's address***].

_(signature line)_______________
[***Name***]

FORM 7 – NOTICE OF SUPPLEMENTAL AUTHORITY

IN THE DISTRICT COURT OF APPEAL,
__________ DISTRICT

[***APPELLANT***],
Appellant,
v. Case No.:____________

STATE OF FLORIDA,
Appellee.
____________________/

NOTICE OF SUPPLEMENTAL AUTHORITY

[***APPELLANT***] hereby submits as supplemental authority the decision of [***give citation to legal authority***]. (attached). This decision is submitted as authority in connection with the appellant's argument regarding [***specify the appellate claim to which the supplemental authority relates***].

_(signature line)______________
[***Name, DC#, Address***]

CERTIFICATE OF SERVICE

I HEREBY CERTIFY that a true copy of the foregoing has been furnished by regular U.S. Mail, this [***date***], to the Office of the Attorney General, [***Attorney General's address***].

_(signature line)______________
[***Name***]

FORM 8 – MOTION TO SUPPLEMENT THE RECORD ON APPEAL

IN THE DISTRICT COURT OF APPEAL,
__________ DISTRICT

[***APPELLANT***],
Appellant,
v. Case No.:____________

STATE OF FLORIDA,
Appellee.
____________________/

MOTION TO SUPPLEMENT THE RECORD ON APPEAL

[***APPELLANT***] hereby respectfully moves this Honorable Court for an order allowing him to supplement the record on appeal pursuant to Rule 9.200(f)(2), and states:

1. [***APPELLANT***] is appealing the denial, after an evidentiary hearing, of his Florida Rule of Criminal Procedure 3.850 Motion for Post Conviction Relief.

2. The Record on Appeal was prepared and transmitted by the lower court on or about [***date***].

3. After having reviewed the Record on Appeal as it pertains to the instant case, [***APPELLANT***] submits that the Record on Appeal needs to be supplemented so as to provide a complete rendition of the facts of [***APPELLANT's***] case to this Honorable Court.

4. It is respectfully submitted that the Record on Appeal should be supplemented to include [***specify portion of the lower court record that needs to be included in the record on appeal***].

5. The above-addressed records directly relate to the claims that were raised at [***APPELLANT's***] 3.850 evidentiary hearing. The issue(s) presented in the instant appeal cannot be resolved without reference to the materials that are the subject of this Motion to Supplement the Record.

6. As authority for this motion, the appellant relies on Rule 9.200(f)(2), which provides in material part that "no proceeding shall be determined because the record is incomplete until an opportunity to supplement the record has been

given." According to this rule, the court must allow the moving party an opportunity to supplement the record. Brice v. State, 419 So.2d 749 (Fla. 2d DCA 1982); Starks v. Starks, 423 So.2d 452 (Fla. 1st DCA 1982).

WHEREFORE, the Appellant respectfully moves for an order allowing him to supplement the record on appeal with [***specify portion of the lower court record that needs to be included in the record on appeal***].

_(signature line)________________
[***Name, DC#, Address***]

CERTIFICATE OF SERVICE

I HEREBY CERTIFY that a true copy of the foregoing has been furnished by regular U.S. Mail, this [***date***], to the Office of the Attorney General, [***Attorney General's address***].

_(signature line)________________
[***Name***]

FORM 9 – MOTION TO EXCEED PAGE LIMIT IN BRIEF

IN THE DISTRICT COURT OF APPEAL,
__________ DISTRICT

[*APPELLANT*],
Appellant,
v. Case No.:____________

STATE OF FLORIDA,
Appellee.
____________________/

MOTION TO EXCEED 50 PAGE LIMIT FOR INITIAL BRIEF

[***APPELLANT***], pursuant to Florida Rule of Appellate Procedure 9.210(a)(5), hereby requests permission to file an initial brief in excess of fifty (50) pages, and states:

1. The instant appeal is from the denial of a Rule 3.850 Motion for Postconviction relief, after an evidentiary hearing.

2. The procedural history of [***APPELLANT's***], case is lengthy and involved. ***[provide detailed procedural history up to point of current appeal]***.

[***and/or***]

3. There are multiple issues involved in the instant case which are unusually complex and require in-depth analysis, thus necessitating an enlargement of the page limit for an initial brief. [***provide brief statement summarizing issues and explaining their complexity***].

[***and/or***]

4. [***Explain any additional factors that justify a request for an enlargement of the page limit***].

5. As a result of the above, Appellant respectfully submits that the merits of [***APPELLANT's***] appeal cannot be adequately addressed within the fifty-page limit imposed by Florida Rule of 9.210.

WHEREFORE, Appellant respectfully requests that this Honorable Court grant the Appellant permission to exceed the fifty-page limit for an initial brief.

_(signature line)________________
[***Name, DC#, Address***]

CERTIFICATE OF SERVICE

I HEREBY CERTIFY that a true copy of the foregoing has been furnished by regular U.S. Mail, this [***date***], to the Office of the Attorney General, [***Attorney General's address***].

_(signature line)________________
[***Name***]

FORM 10 – VOLUNTARY DISMISSAL OF APPEAL

IN THE DISTRICT COURT OF APPEAL,
__________ DISTRICT

[***APPELLANT***],
Appellant,
v. Case No.:______________

STATE OF FLORIDA,
Appellee.
_____________________/

NOTICE OF VOLUNTARY DISMISSAL

Appellant hereby voluntarily dismisses this appeal pursuant to Florida Rule of Appellate Procedure 9.350(b).

_(signature line)________________
[***Name, DC#, Address***]

CERTIFICATE OF SERVICE

I HEREBY CERTIFY that a true copy of the foregoing has been furnished by regular U.S. Mail, this [***date***], to the Office of the Attorney General, [***Attorney General's address***].

_(signature line)________
[***Name***]

FORM 11 – INITIAL APPELLATE BRIEF

IN THE DISTRICT COURT OF APPEAL,
__________ DISTRICT

[***APPELLANT***],
Appellant,
v. Case No.:______________

STATE OF FLORIDA,
Appellee.
____________________/

AN APPEAL FROM THE __________ JUDICIAL CIRCUIT
COURT, IN AND FOR ______________ COUNTY

THE HONORABLE ***[JUDGE'S NAME]***
PRESIDING JUDGE OF THE CIRCUIT COURT

APPELLANT'S INITIAL BRIEF

[Appellant's name, DC number, address]

****

TABLE OF CONTENTS

Preliminary Statement iv
Table of Citations vi
Statement of Case and Facts 1
Summary of the Argument 24
Standard of Review 25
Issue One
THE LOWER COURT WAS IN ERROR IN DENYING APPELLANT'S 3850 MOTION; [***specify reason denial of 3850 motion was in error***] 31
Conclusion 38
Certificate of Service 40
Certificate of Font and Type Size 40

****

PRELIMINARY STATEMENT

The instant appeal is one from the denial of a Florida Rule of Criminal Procedure 3.850 Motion for Post Conviction Relief. Any references to the record on appeal will be cited by volume number followed by "R" and the corresponding page number(s), i.e., (V.1,R.1).

The transcripts of Appellant's trial are included in volumes 3 through 8 of the record on appeal. Any references to the trial transcripts shall be cited by record volume number, followed by the original trial transcript page numbers, i.e., (V.3, T.1).

The Appellant will be referred to herein as "Mr. Doe" or "John."

****

TABLE OF CITATIONS

[with cases listed alphabetically, statutes and other authorities, and the pages of the brief on which each citation appears]

CASE	PAGE
Atkins v. Attorney General, 932 F.2d 1430 (11th Cir. 1991)	32
Henry v. Scully, 78 F.3d 51 (2nd Cir 1996)	32
Johnston v. Moore, 789 So.2d 262 (Fla. 2001)	26
Johnson v. Singletary, 647 So.2d 106 (Fla.1994)	27
Jones v. State, 709 So.2d 512 (Fla. 1998)	26,27
State v. Spaziano, 692 So.2d 174 (Fla.1997)	27
Stephens v. State, 748 So.2d 1028 (Fla.1999)	26
Strickland v. Washington, 466 U.S. 668 (1984)	26,32

Florida Statutes

Florida Statutes §825.1025	1

****

STATEMENT OF CASE AND FACTS

The statement of the case and of the facts shall include the nature of the case, the course of the proceedings, and the disposition in the lower tribunal. It should also give a detailed recitation of all facts of record that support the claims raised in the initial brief. References to the appropriate volume and pages of the record or transcript shall be made.

Be sure to summarize the procedural background of the case, including:

- ***charges against defendant (when charged, charged by indictment or information, specific charges and how many counts)***
- ***did defendant go to trial or enter plea?***
- ***date of conviction***
- ***what sentences were imposed and on what date?***
- ***date that appeal was decided and date of appellate mandate***
- ***date of 3.850 filing***
- ***issues presented in 3.850 motion***
- ***when did denial of 3.850 occur?***
- ***was 3.850 summarily denied or did denial occur after evidentiary hearing?***
- ***trial court's rationale for denying 3.850 motion.***

SUMMARY OF THE ARGUMENT

[***Give A summary of the argument, condensing succinctly, accurately, and clearly the argument actually made in the body of the brief. It should not be a mere repetition of the headings under which the argument is arranged. It should seldom exceed 2 and never 5 pages***].

STANDARD OF REVIEW

The claim submitted herein addresses a deprivation of Appellant's Sixth Amendment right to effective assistance of counsel. An ineffective assistance of counsel claim is a mixed question of law and fact, subject to plenary review based on Strickland v. Washington, 466 U.S. 668 (1984). See, Johnston v. Moore, 789 So.2d 262 (Fla. 2001). With a mixed question of fact and law, the appellate court must give deference to the trial court's findings of historical fact but the ultimate mixed question of law and fact is subject to independent appellate review. Way v. State, 760 So.2d 903 (Fla. 2000); and, Stephens v. State, 748 So.2d 1028 (Fla.1999).

ISSUE

THE LOWER COURT WAS IN ERROR IN DENYING APPELLANT'S 3.850 MOTION; [***specify reason denial of 3.850 motion was in error***].

[***Provide legal argument on claims that addresses the proper legal standards and citations of authority, and applies said standards to the facts that support the appellate claims***].

CONCLUSION

Based upon the foregoing arguments and citations of authority, it is clear that Appellant was deprived of his constitutional right to effective assistance of counsel. The lower court was, therefore, in error in denying postconviction relief on the claims addressed herein.

WHEREFORE, it is respectfully requested that this Honorable Court vacate Appellant's judgment and sentence and remand the instant case to the trial court for the purpose of conducting a new trial; or in the alternative grant any other such relief that this Court deems proper and just.

_(signature line)______________
[***Name, DC#, Address***]

CERTIFICATE OF SERVICE

I HEREBY CERTIFY that a true copy of the foregoing has been furnished by regular U.S. Mail, this [***date***], to the Office of the Attorney General, [***Attorney General's address***].

_(signature line)______________
[***Name***]

FORM 12 – REQUEST FOR ORAL ARGUMENT

IN THE DISTRICT COURT OF APPEAL,
__________ DISTRICT

[***APPELLANT***],
Appellant,
v. Case No.:______________

STATE OF FLORIDA,
Appellee.
______________________/

REQUEST FOR ORAL ARGUMENT

[***APPELLANT***] hereby requests oral argument, pursuant to Florida Rule of Appellate Procedure 9.320, in the instant case. It is respectfully submitted that oral argument will be helpful to the court in reviewing the claims at issue.

_(signature line)________________
[***Name, DC#, Address***]

CERTIFICATE OF SERVICE

I HEREBY CERTIFY that a true copy of the foregoing has been furnished by regular U.S. Mail, this [***date***], to the Office of the Attorney General, [***Attorney General's address***].

_(signature line)________________
[***Name***]

FORM 13 – MOTION FOR REHEARING

IN THE DISTRICT COURT OF APPEAL,
__________ DISTRICT

[***APPELLANT***],
Appellant,
v. Case No.:_____________

STATE OF FLORIDA,
Appellee.
____________________/

MOTION FOR REHEARING

[***APPELLANT***] hereby moves this Honorable Court for Rehearing pursuant to Florida Rule of Appellate Procedure 9.330, and states:

1. On [***date***], this Honorable Court entered a written opinion in the instant case, which affirmed the lower court's denial of the Appellant's Rule 3.850 Motion for Postconviction Relief.

2. It is respectfully submitted that this Honorable Court may have overlooked or misapprehended pertinent facts **and/or** points of law of the instant case.

3. [***Specify facts and/or points of law that the court misapprehended or overlooked and explain how this improperly affected the court's opinion***].

WHEREFORE, [***APPELLANT***] respectfully moves this Honorable Court for an order granting rehearing, pursuant to Rule 9.330(a), and:

1. Reverse the lower court's denial of Appellant's 3.850 motion; and,

2. Vacate Appellant's judgment and sentence and remand the instant caseto the trial court for the purpose of conducting a new trial; or in the alternative,

3. Grant any other relief that this Court deems just and proper.

_(signature line)_______________
[***Name, DC#, Address***]

CERTIFICATE OF SERVICE

I HEREBY CERTIFY that a true copy of the foregoing has been furnished by regular U.S. Mail, this [***date***], to the Office of the Attorney General, [***Attorney General's address***].

_(signature line)________________
[***Name***]

FORM 14 – MOTION FOR WRITTEN OPINION

IN THE DISTRICT COURT OF APPEAL,
__________ DISTRICT

[***APPELLANT***],
Appellant,
v. Case No.:____________

STATE OF FLORIDA,
Appellee.
____________________/

MOTION FOR WRITTEN OPINION

[***APPELLANT***] hereby moves this Honorable Court for a written opinion in the instant case, pursuant to Florida Rule of Appellate Procedure 9.330(a), and states:

1. On or about [***date***], [***APPELLANT***] filed a Rule 3.850 Motion with the lower court.

2. [***APPELLANT's***] 3.850 denied by the lower court on [***date***].

3. On [***date***], this Honorable court issued a *per curiam* opinion affirming the lower court's denial of relief. No written opinion was provided.

4. For the purposes of rehearing/clarification, Appellant cannot specifically state which issues of fact or law this Court may have overlooked or misapprehended since no written opinion was provided. Nevertheless, it is respectfully submitted that it appears that if this Honorable Court would provide a written opinion for the affirmance, such an opinion would be in direct and express conflict with opinions of the Florida Supreme Court and other district courts addressing similar issues. As such, Appellant requests that this Court render a written opinion in the instant case.

5. The issue from Appellant's 3.850 motion that was addressed in the instant appeal was as follows: [***specify issue***].

6. The above issue was based upon case law from the Florida Supreme Court and other judicial districts of Florida, to wit: [***specify caselaw that claim is based upon***]. It is respectfully submitted that application of the aforementioned

authorities to the factual scenario in Appellant's case should have resulted in postconviction relief for [***APPELLANT***].

7. As this Court's *per curiam* affirmance provided no written opinion, it is impossible to specifically address what points of fact or law this Honorable Court may have overlooked or misapprehended. Nevertheless, it is respectfully submitted that the denial of relief in the instant case appears to be in direct conflict with the above-cited caselaw.

8. If this Court's decision is in fact in direct conflict with the above legal authorities, then such conflict would provide a legitimate basis for Florida Supreme Court review. The Florida Supreme Court has discretionary jurisdiction over decisions of district courts which "expressly and directly conflict with a decision of another district court of appeal or of the supreme court on the same question of law." Fla.R.App.P 9.030(a)(2)(a)(iv).

WHEREFORE, Appellant respectfully requests that this Honorable Court grant this motion and issue a written opinion addressing the issues raised in the instant appeal.

_(signature line)________________
[***Name, DC#, Address***]

CERTIFICATE OF SERVICE

I HEREBY CERTIFY that a true copy of the foregoing has been furnished by regular U.S. Mail, this [***date***], to the Office of the Attorney General, [***Attorney General's address***].

_(signature line)________________
[***Name***]

FORM 15 – MOTION FOR CERTIFICATION

IN THE DISTRICT COURT OF APPEAL,
__________ DISTRICT

[***APPELLANT***],
Appellant,
v. Case No.:_____________

STATE OF FLORIDA,
Appellee.
____________________/

MOTION FOR CERTIFICATION

[***APPELLANT***] moves for an order certifying that the decision in this case conflicts with decisions of the ___ District Court of Appeal. In support of the motion, Appellant states:

1. This Honorable Court's opinion affirming the lower court's denial of postconviction relief, is in conflict with [***case citation***].

2. [***Explain how the case conflicts with an opinion of another district court of appeal***].

3. Although the decision in the instant case is in conflict with [***case citation***], a decision of another district court of appeal, the Court has not certified conflict in the present case.

WHEREFORE, the Appellant respectfully requests that this Court enter an Order certifying that the decision in the instant case conflicts with the above-cited decision of the ____ District Court of Appeal.

_(signature line)_______________
[***Name, DC#, Address***]

CERTIFICATE OF SERVICE

I HEREBY CERTIFY that a true copy of the foregoing has been furnished by regular U.S. Mail, this [***date***], to the Office of the Attorney General, [***Attorney General's address***].

_(signature line)_______________
[***Name***]

FORM 16 – NOTICE TO INVOKE DISCRETIONARY JURISDICTION OF FLORIDA SUPREME COURT

IN THE DISTRICT COURT OF APPEAL,
__________ DISTRICT

[***APPELLANT***],
Appellant,
v. Case No.:_____________

STATE OF FLORIDA,
Appellee.
_____________________/

NOTICE TO INVOKE DISCRETIONARY JURISDICTION

NOTICE IS GIVEN that [***APPELLANT***] invokes the discretionary jurisdiction of the Florida Supreme Court to review the decision of this court rendered on [***date***].

The decision is within the discretionary jurisdiction of the Florida Supreme Court, pursuant to Article V Section 3(b)[***specify sub-subsection***] of the Florida Constitution, because [***specify one of the jurisdictional bases listed in Article V Section 3(b)of the Florida Constitution***].

Dated this ____ day of _________, 20__.

_(signature line)_______________
[***Name, DC#, Address***]

CERTIFICATE OF SERVICE

I HEREBY CERTIFY that a true copy of the foregoing has been furnished by regular U.S. Mail, this [***date***], to the Office of the Attorney General, [***Attorney General's address***].

_(signature line)_______________
[***Name***]

FORM 17 – RULE 3.850 MOTION FOR POSTCONVICTION RELIEF AND SUPPORTING MEMORANDUM

IN THE CIRCUIT COURT OF THE ________ JUDICIAL CIRCUIT,
IN AND FOR ____________ COUNTY, FLORIDA

[***DEFENDANT***],

v. Case No.:______________

STATE OF FLORIDA.
_____________________/

MOTION FOR POST CONVICTION RELIEF
AND SUPPORTING MEMORANDUM

[***DEFENDANT***], pursuant to Florida Rule of Criminal Procedure 3.850, hereby moves this Honorable Court for an order vacating his judgment and sentence in the instant case, and states:

1. Name and location of the court that entered the judgment of conviction under attack:

2. Date of judgment of conviction:

3. Length of sentence:

4. Nature of offense(s) involved (all counts):

5. What was your plea? (check only one)
   (a) Not guilty ____
   (b) Guilty ____
   (c) Nolo contendere ____
   (d) Not guilty by reason of insanity ____

If you entered one plea to one count and a different plea to another count, give details:

6. Kind of trial: (check only one):
   (a) Jury ____
   (b) Judge only without jury ____

7. Did you testify at the trial or at any pretrial hearing?
Yes ________ No ________
If yes, list each such occasion:

8. Did you appeal from the judgment of conviction?
Yes ________ No ________

9. If you did appeal, answer the following:
(a) Name of court:
(b) Result:
(c) Date of result:
(d) Citation (if known):

10. Other than a direct appeal from the judgment of conviction and sentence, have you previously filed any petitions, applications, motions, etc., with respect to this judgment in this court?
Yes ________ No ________

11. If your answer to number 10 was "yes," give the following information (applies only to proceedings in this court):
(a)(1) Nature of the proceeding:
(2) Grounds raised:
(3) Did you receive an evidentiary hearing on your petition, application, motion, etc.?
Yes ________ No ________
(4) Result:
(5) Date of result:

(b) As to any second petition, application, motion, etc., give the same information:
(1) Nature of the proceeding:
(2) Grounds raised:
(3) Did you receive an evidentiary hearing on your petition, application, motion, etc.?
Yes ________ No ________
(4) Result:
(5) Date of result:

12. Other than a direct appeal from the judgment of conviction and sentence, have you previously filed any petitions, applications, motions, etc., with respect to this judgment in any other court?
Yes ________ No ________

13. If your answer to number 12 was "yes," give the following information:
(a) (1) Name of court:
(2) Nature of the proceeding:
(3) Grounds raised:
(4) Did you receive an evidentiary hearing on your petition, application, motion, etc.?
Yes ________ No ________
(5) Result:
(6) Date of result:

14. State concisely every ground on which you claim that the judgment or sentence is unlawful. Summarize briefly the facts supporting each ground.

A. Ground 1:

Supporting FACTS (tell your story briefly without citing cases or law):

B. Ground 2:

Supporting FACTS (tell your story briefly without citing cases or law):

15. Do you have any petition, application, appeal, motion, etc., now pending in any court, either state or federal, as to the judgment under attack?
Yes ________ No ________

16. If your answer to number 15 was "yes," give the following information:
(a) Name of court:
(b) Nature of the proceeding:
(c) Grounds raised:
(d) Status of the proceedings:

17. Give the name and address, if known, of each attorney who represented you in the following stages of the judgment attacked herein.
(a) At preliminary hearing:
(b) At arraignment and plea:
(c) At trial:
(d) At sentencing:
(e) On appeal:
(f) In any postconviction proceeding:
(g) On appeal from any adverse ruling in a postconviction proceeding:

MEMORANDUM OF LAW

STATEMENT OF THE FACTS : [***In this section, provide a detailed factual scenario that supports any claims asserted in the motion. Be specific with citation to trial transcripts, record portions, depositions, and any other documentation used to support the postconviction claims***].

INEFFECTIVE ASSISTANCE OF COUNSEL - THE *STRICKLAND* STANDARD

In the instant motion, it is asserted that defense counsel rendered ineffective assistance of counsel. In order to demonstrate ineffective assistance of counsel a defendant must prove both that his counsel performed deficiently and that the performance actually prejudiced the defendant. Strickland v. Washington, 466 U.S. 668 (1984). The two prongs of the ineffectiveness inquiry are independent of one another, and thus, must both be proved to establish a claim of ineffective assistance of counsel. Id. at 697. In order to satisfy the "performance" prong of the Strickland test a defendant must show that his counsel's representation fell below an objective standard of reasonableness. Id. at 687-688. In order to demonstrate the prejudice prong of Strickland "the defendant must show that there is a reasonable probability that, but for counsel's unprofessional errors, the result of the proceeding would have been different." Id. at 694. A reasonable probability is a probability sufficient to undermine confidence in the outcome. Id. In Lockhart v. Fretwell, 506 U.S. 364 (1993), The United States Supreme Court further explained that "the 'prejudice' component of the Strickland test...focuses on the question whether counsel's deficient performance renders the result of the trial unreliable or the proceedings fundamentally unfair." *See also*, Young v. Catoe, 205 F.3d 750, 759 (4th Cir. 2000) [it need not be proved that counsel's performance more likely than not affected the outcome of the case, instead, the petitioner need only demonstrate "a probability sufficient to undermine confidence in the outcome."]

ISSUE ONE

[***DEFENDANT***] WAS DEPRIVED OF HIS CONSTITUTIONAL RIGHT TO EFFECTIVE ASSISTANCE OF COUNSEL WHEN HIS ATTORNEY FAILED TO [***briefly summarize act of attorney that amounts to ineffectiveness of counsel***].

[***Here present caselaw/legal authority that supports your claim and then apply the facts of your case to the legal authorities to demonstrate why relief is due***].

CONCLUSION

Based upon the foregoing arguments and citations of authority, it is clear that [***Briefly** reiterate all claims addressed in the motion*]. As such, [***DEFENDANT's***] judgment and sentence should be vacated and a new trial should be granted.

WHEREFORE, [***DEFENDANT***] respectfully moves this court to:

1. Grant this Motion for Post Conviction Relief, vacate the judgment and sentence as entered, and remand this cause for *de novo* jury trial proceedings; or, in the alternative,

2. Order the Respondent to show cause as to why this Motion should not be granted; and thereafter, prior to the adjudication of this motion,

3. Order a full and fair evidentiary hearing with [***DEFENDANT***] present and represented by counsel, in order for [***DEFENDANT***] to sustain, if necessary, his burden of proof and persuasion; or in the alternative,

4. Grant any other or further relief as this Court deems necessary in the interest of justice.

_(signature line)_______________
[***Name, DC#, Address***]

CERTIFICATE OF SERVICE

I HEREBY CERTIFY that a true copy of the foregoing has been furnished by regular U.S. Mail, this [***date***], to the Office of the State Attorney, [***State Attorney's address***].

_(signature line)_______________
[***Name***]

OATH

Under penalties of perjury, I declare that I have read the foregoing motion and that the facts stated in it are true.

_(signature line)_______________
[***Name***]

CERTIFICATION OF ENGLISH LANGUAGE

I hereby certify that I understand English.

_(signature line)________________
[***Name***]

[OR]

CERTIFICATION OF NON-ENGLISH LANGUAGE AND TRANSLATION

I hereby certify that I cannot understand English, and that I have had the instant motion translated completely into [***language that the defendant understands***] by [***name of translator***].

_(signature line)________________
[***Name***]

CERTIFICATION OF TRANSLATION

I hereby certify I have provided an accurate and complete translation of the instant motion into [***language that the defendant understands***] to [***DEFENDANT***].

_(signature line)________________
[***Name and Address of Translator***]

FORM 18 – MOTION TO FILE BELATED 3.850 MOTION

IN THE CIRCUIT COURT OF THE ________ JUDICIAL CIRCUIT,
IN AND FOR ____________ COUNTY, FLORIDA

[***DEFENDANT***],

v. Case No.:______________

STATE OF FLORIDA.
_____________________/

PETITION FOR WRIT OF HABEAS CORPUS

[***DEFENDANT***], pursuant to Rules 3.850(b)(3), Florida Rules of Criminal Procedure, respectfully petitions this Honorable Court to issue a writ of habeas corpus directed to the Respondent, STATE OF FLORIDA, through the Office of the State Attorney for the ______ Judicial Circuit, in and for ______ County, affording Petitioner permission to file a belated Rule 3.850 Motion in the above-captioned case. In support thereof, he shows as follows:

1. On [***date***], the Petitioner was found guilty in _________ County Circuit Court case number_____________, of the following offenses: [***specify offenses***].

2. On [***date***], [***DEFENDANT***] was sentenced to [***specify sentences***].

3. [***DEFENDANT***] timely appealed his judgment and sentence to the ____ District Court of Appeal. [***DEFENDANT's***] judgment and sentence was affirmed on [***date***]. The Mandate was issued on [***date***].

4. [***List any postconviction/collateral petitions or motions that have already been filed and disposed of***].

5. No other postconviction motions or petitions have been filed in this or any other court with regard to the instant case .

6. [***DEFENDANT***] seeks entry of a writ of habeas corpus affording him the opportunity to file a belated Rule 3.850 Motion in the instant case.

STATEMENT OF FACTS UPON WHICH THIS PETITION IS BASED

Subsequent to his direct appeal, [***DEFENDANT***] retained the services of

[***ATTORNEY***]. [***ATTORNEY***] was formally retained on [***DEFENDANT's***] behalf on [***date***]. [***DEFENDANT***] paid the agreed-upon fee of _______ for [***ATTORNEY's***] services. (Attached is a copy of the retainer agreement). [***ATTORNEY***] was specifically retained to timely file a Rule 3.850 postconviction motion for [***DEFENDANT***]. Contrary to his contractual obligation to [***DEFENDANT***], [***ATTORNEY***] failed to timely file a Rule 3.850 motion for [***DEFENDANT***].

[***Provide any additional information that demonstrates that retained legal counsel failed to timely file a 3.850 motion***].

ISSUE

[***DEFENDANT***], IS ENTITLED TO FILE A BELATED RULE 3.850 MOTION FOR POSTCONVICTION RELIEF DUE TO THE FAILURE OF HIS RETAINED ATTORNEY TO TIMELY FILE A POSTCONVICTION ATTACK ON THE JUDGMENT AND SENTENCE IN THE INSTANT CASE.

It is true that a criminal defendant does not have a due process right, pursuant to the Sixth Amendment of the United States Constitution, to effective assistance of counsel in a post conviction proceeding. Lambrix v. State, 698 So.2d 247 (Fla. 1996). However, the holding of Lambrix does not dictate that a post conviction movant is to receive no due process whatsoever. In fact, it was held in State v. Weeks, 166 So.2d 892 (Fla. 1964), that "[postconviction] remedies are subject to the more flexible standards of due process announced in the Fifth Amendment, Constitution of the United States." Weeks at 896. For example, in Weeks and Graham v. State, 372 So.2d 1363 (Fla. 1979), the Florida Supreme Court held that due process required the appointment of postconviction counsel when a prisoner filed a substantially meritorious postconviction motion and a hearing on the motion was potentially so complex that the assistance of counsel was needed. Thus, although a postconviction movant may not have the right to effective postconviction counsel pursuant to the Sixth Amendment of the United States Constitution, said movant shall still be afforded the more flexible standards of due process.

In Steele v. Kehoe, 747 So.2d 931 (Fla. 1999), the Florida Supreme Court addressed a situation similar to the instant case and found that the defendant was due relief pursuant to the more flexible standards of due process announced in the Fifth Amendment of the United States Constitution. In Steele, William Steele was convicted of first degree murder and sentenced to life in prison. Id. Mr. Steele claimed that he retained attorney Kehoe to file a motion for postconviction relief pursuant to Florida Rule of Criminal Procedure 3.850, and that said attorney did not file a timely post conviction motion on Steele's behalf. Id. at 932. Mr. Steele's *pro se* rule 3.850 motions were rejected by the trial court and the Fifth District Court of Appeal because they were filed after the two-year deadline had expired. Id.

As a result of his post conviction actions being barred, Steele filed a legal malpractice complaint against Kehoe. But, since Steele's 3.850 motions had been dismissed, Steele did not have an opportunity to demonstrate that he was improperly convicted as a result of his attorney's negligence. Id. The trial court dismissed Steele's complaint because he could not prove his actual innocence or that his underlying conviction had been set aside. Id.

The dismissal of Steele's complaint was affirmed by the 5th District Court of Appeal because exoneration is a prerequisite to a legal malpractice action arising from a criminal conviction. Id. However, the 5th District was troubled by the result, noting that irrespective of its holding, a monetary remedy in a civil action would be inadequate to redress Steele's injury. And, although the court recognized that, pursuant to Lambrix v. State 698 So.2d 247 (Fla. 1996), Steele had no right to effective postconviction counsel, they did consider what other possible remedies were available. The District Court considered what remedies would be available to a prisoner who hired an attorney to pursue postconviction relief and said attorney failed to timely file a motion within the two year period. The District Court held that "[i]f a prisoner is denied the opportunity to challenge his conviction under an appropriate rule only because of the negligence of his attorney, then due process requires a belated filing procedure similar to that allowed in belated appeals." Steele v. Kehoe, 724 So.2d 1192 (Fla. 5th DCA 1998).

On appeal, the Florida Supreme Court in Steele v. Kehoe, 747 So.2d 931 (Fla. 1999), agreed with the District Court, stating that "...**due process** entitles a prisoner to a hearing on a claim that he or she missed the deadline to file a rule 3.850 motion because his or her attorney had agreed to file the motion but failed to do so in a timely manner." Id. at 934 (*emphasis added*). As such, the Florida Supreme Court held that the correct procedure would be for the trial court to conduct a hearing on whether Kehoe undertook to file a 3.850 motion on Steele's behalf, but failed to timely file the motion. And, if such circumstances are proven, then the right to file a belated 3.850 motion should be granted.

As a result of Steele v. Kehoe, 724 So.2d 1192 (Fla. 5th DCA 1998), Florida Rule of Criminal Procedure 3.850(b) was amended to provide a new exception to the two-year period of limitations for filing a Rule 3.850 Motion. Rule 3.850(b)(3) now provides that an exception to the two-year period of limitations occurs when "the defendant retained counsel to timely file a 3.850 motion and counsel, through neglect, failed to file the motion."

The facts in the instant case are similar to the facts in Steele. Subsequent to his judgment and sentence, [***DEFENDANT***] hired [***ATTORNEY***] to file a postconviction motion for [***DEFENDANT***]. The two-year period of limitations in [***DEFENDANT's***] case ended on [***date***] (two years from the mandate of his direct appeal). [***ATTORNEY***] was retained on [***date***] and was thus retained well before the two-year period of limitations lapsed. Unfortunately, [***ATTORNEY***] failed to timely file [***DEFENDANT's***] Rule 3.850 motion prior to the expiration of the two-year period of limitations. [***DEFENDANT***] is now well outside of the two-year period of limitations for filing a Rule 3.850 motion.

Pursuant to Steele v. Kehoe, 747 So.2d 931 (Fla. 1999), due process entitles [***DEFENDANT***] to a hearing on the claim that he missed the deadline to file a Rule 3.850 motion because his attorney agreed to file the motion but failed to do so in a timely manner. Id. at 934. The Florida Supreme Court held that in such a situation the correct procedure would be for the trial court to conduct a hearing on whether the attorney undertook to file a 3.850 motion on [***DEFENDANT's***] behalf, but failed to timely file the motion. And, if such circumstances are proven, then the right to file a belated 3.850 motion should be granted to [***DEFENDANT***].

WHEREFORE, [***DEFENDANT***] respectfully requests that this Honorable Court grant this petition and order that an evidentiary hearing be held to determine whether or not [***DEFENDANT***] should be granted permission to file a belated Rule 3.850 Motion for Postconviction Relief, and, thereafter, grant [***DEFENDANT***] permission to file a belated Rule 3.850 Motion for Postconviction Relief.

_(signature line)_______________
[***Name, DC#, Address***]

CERTIFICATE OF SERVICE

I HEREBY CERTIFY that a true copy of the foregoing has been furnished by regular U.S. Mail, this [***date***], to the Office of the State Attorney, [***State Attorney's address***].

_(signature line)_______________
[***Name***]

FORM 19 – MOTION TO LIMIT SCOPE OF USE OF TESTIMONY AND EVIDENCE PROFFERED AT EVIDENTIARY HEARING

IN THE CIRCUIT COURT OF THE ________ JUDICIAL CIRCUIT,
IN AND FOR ___________ COUNTY, FLORIDA

[***DEFENDANT***],

v. Case No.:____________

STATE OF FLORIDA.
____________________/

MOTION TO LIMIT SCOPE OF USE OF TESTIMONY AND EVIDENCE PROFFERED AT EVIDENTIARY HEARING

[***DEFENDANT***] hereby files this motion to limit the use of the testimony and evidence elicited at the 3.850 evidentiary hearing in the instant case to the instant collateral proceedings, and states:

1. [***DEFENDANT***] currently has pending a Rule 3.850 Motion for Postconviction Relief in the above-captioned case.

2. An evidentiary hearing is scheduled for [***DEFENDANT's***] 3.850 Motion on [***date***].

3. As the issues before the Court involve questions of attorney ineffectiveness, [***DEFENDANT***] must waive his attorney-client privilege relating to his trial attorney, [***Attorney Name***]. *See*, Lopez v. Singletery, 634 So.2d 1054 (Fla. 1993).

4. Further, to satisfy his burden of proof, [***DEFENDANT***] may need to testify at his evidentiary hearing.

5. While the testimony of [***DEFENDANT***] and [***ATTORNEY***] are clearly relevant to the claims under consideration by the Court, the applicability of said evidence should be limited solely to the current proceedings before this Court. In other words, it would be fundamentally unfair to allow any evidence adduced in the current proceedings to be later used against [***DEFENDANT***] in a new trial (should one be granted).

6. The waiver of [***DEFENDANT's***] attorney-client privilege only occurs because of the claims of ineffectiveness of counsel. Should this court grant

[***DEFENDANT's***] 3.850 motion and vacate his judgment and sentence based upon a finding of ineffectiveness of trial counsel, [***DEFENDANT***] should be placed in the position that he was prior to trial, i.e., that no privileged material should be allowed to be presented against him.

7. As a result of the above [***DEFENDANT***] moves this Court to hold that the waiver of his attorney-client privilege and his right to remain silent, be construed narrowly so as to preclude use of confidential information at a new trial or retrial (should such a trial be granted). In Bittaker v. Woodford, 331 F.3d 715 (9th Cir. 2003), it was held that the scope of a habeas petitioner's waiver arising from a claim of ineffective assistance of counsel, raised in a habeas petition, extended only to litigation of the federal habeas petition; and, therefore, attorney-client privilege was not waived for all time and all purposes, including the possible retrial of the petitioner, if he was successful in setting aside his original conviction or sentence. Likewise, addressing the same issue, U.S. v. Pinson, 584 F.3d 972, 978 (10th Cir. 2009) held that a court must impose a waiver no broader than needed to ensure the fairness of the proceedings before it.

8. Also, in Simmons v. U.S., 390 U.S. 377, 394, 88 S.Ct. 967, 976 (1968) it was noted that where testimony of the defendant was required to support a 4th Amendment suppression claim, an undeniable tension is created between the protection against illegal searches and seizures and the 5th Amendment protection against self-incrimination and, therefore, "when a defendant testifies in support of a motion to suppress evidence on Fourth Amendment grounds, his testimony may not thereafter be admitted against him at trial on the issue of guilt unless he makes no objection." The instant case presents a similar dilemma for [***DEFENDANT***]; in order to support his burden of proof about ineffectiveness of his attorney, [***DEFENDANT***] may have to testify and thus be subjected to questions about his case. If said testimony of [***DEFENDANT***] would later be used against him at a retrial, then a tension is created between [***DEFENDANT's***] 5th Amendment right to remain silent and his ability to adequately pursue his 6th Amendment right to effective assistance of counsel. Just as with Simmons, such a dilemma should be remedied by limiting the use of [***DEFENDANT's***] testimony to the instant collateral proceedings and precluding any use of his testimony at a retrial.

WHEREFORE, [***DEFENDANT***] respectfully requests that this Honorable Court grant this motion and enter an Order: (1) limiting the use of any material protected by attorney-client privilege to the instant matter and barring use of said material at any retrial; and, (2) limiting the use of any testimony from [***DEFENDANT***] to the instant matter and barring use of said material at any retrial.

_(signature line)_______________
[***Name, DC#, Address***]

CERTIFICATE OF SERVICE

I HEREBY CERTIFY that a true copy of the foregoing has been furnished by regular U.S. Mail, this [***date***], to the Office of the State Attorney, [***State Attorney's address***].

_(signature line)________________
[***Name***]

FORM 20 – MOTION FOR COURT TO RULE ON MOVANT'S MOTION FOR POSTCONVICTION RELIEF

IN THE CIRCUIT COURT OF THE ________ JUDICIAL CIRCUIT,
IN AND FOR ___________ COUNTY, FLORIDA

[***DEFENDANT***],

v. Case No.:____________

STATE OF FLORIDA.
____________________/

MOTION FOR COURT TO RULE ON MOVANT'S MOTION FOR POSTCONVICTION RELIEF

[***DEFENDANT***] respectfully moves this Honorable Court to rule on [***DEFENDANT's***] Florida Rule of Criminal Procedure 3.850 Motion for Post Conviction Relief, and states:

1. On or about [***date***], [***DEFENDANT***] filed a Florida Rule of Criminal Procedure 3.850 Motion for Postconviction Relief with this Honorable Court.

2. Since the filing of [***DEFENDANT's***] 3.850 motion, this Honorable Court has taken no action on said 3.850.

3. Rule of Judicial Administration 2.215(f) provides that, "Every judge has a duty to rule upon and announce an order or judgment on every matter submitted to that judge within a reasonable time." Rule 2.215(f) establishes a 60 day presumptively reasonable time for ruling on matters in that it provides that, "Each judge shall maintain a log of cases under advisement and inform the chief judge of the circuit at the end of each calendar month of each case that has been held under advisement for more than 60 days." [***DEFENDANT***] respectfully submits that the __ months that [***DEFENDANT's***] 3.850 has been pending before this Court has been a sufficiently reasonable amount of time for the 3.850 motion to be resolved.

WHEREFORE, [***DEFENDANT***] respectfully requests that this Honorable Court:

1. Enter an Order requiring the State to respond to [***DEFENDANT's***] 3.850; and, thereafter,

2. Set this case for an evidentiary hearing on the issues presented in [***DEFENDANT's***] 3.850 motion.

_(signature line)_______________
[***Name, DC#, Address***]

CERTIFICATE OF SERVICE

I HEREBY CERTIFY that a true copy of the foregoing has been furnished by regular U.S. Mail, this [***date***], to the Office of the State Attorney, [***State Attorney's address***].

_(signature line)_______________
[***Name***]

FORM 21 – PETITION FOR WRIT OF MANDAMUS

IN THE DISTRICT COURT OF APPEAL,
__________ DISTRICT

[***PETITIONER***],
Petitioner,
v. Case No.:_____________

STATE OF FLORIDA,
Respondent.
____________________/

PETITION FOR WRIT OF MANDAMUS

Pursuant to Florida Rule of Appellate Procedure 9.100, [***PETITIONER***] respectfully petitions this Honorable Court for a Writ of Mandamus compelling the lower tribunal to issue an Order on [***PETITIONER's***] Florida Rule of Criminal Procedure 3.850 Motion for Post Conviction Relief.

I.
BASIS FOR INVOKING JURISDICTION

This Court has jurisdiction to issue a writ of mandamus under Article V section 4(b)(3) of the Florida Constitution and Rule 9.030(b)(3) of the Florida Rules of Appellate Procedure. Mandamus is the proper remedy where a trial court fails to timely issue an order on a Florida Rule of Criminal Procedure 3.850 Motion for Post Conviction Relief. Browning v. State, 814 So.2d 1220 (Fla. 1st DCA 2002); Kramp v. Fagan, 568 So.2d 479 (Fla. 1st DCA 1990).

II.
STATEMENT OF THE FACTS

On or about [***date***], [***PETITIONER***] filed a Florida Rule of Criminal Procedure 3.850 Motion for Post Conviction Relief with the ___ Judicial Circuit Court, in and for ________ County, Florida, in circuit court case number __________. (Ex.A, attached). [***PETITIONER's***] 3.850 Motion has now been pending before the lower court for [***specify length of pendency***]. To date, no action has been taken by the lower court on [***PETITIONER's***] 3.850.

On or about [***date***], the undersigned filed a Motion for Court to Rule on Movant's Motion for Post-Conviction Relief with the lower court. (Ex.B, attached). On or about [***date***], a courtesy copy of said motion was likewise mailed to the Honorable [***Circuit Judge***], circuit judge of the lower court. (Ex.C, attached). In [***PETITIONER's***] Motion to Rule, the undersigned asserted that the lower court has had a sufficient amount of time to resolve [***PETITIONER's***] 3.850 motion. To date no Order has been issued on [***PETITIONER's***] 3.850 motion by the lower court.

III.
THE NATURE OF THE RELIEF SOUGHT

The nature of the relief sought by this petition is a Writ of Mandamus compelling the Honorable [***Circuit Judge***] of the lower court to issue an order on [***PETITIONER's***] Florida Rule of Criminal Procedure 3.850 Motion for Post Conviction Relief.

IV.
ARGUMENT

Florida Rule of Judicial Administration 2.050(f) provides that "[e]very judge has a duty to rule upon and announce an order or judgment on every matter submitted to that judge within a reasonable time." When a trial judge fails to rule on a motion within a reasonable time, mandamus is the proper remedy. Mason v. Circuit Court, 603 So.2d 94 (Fla. 5th DCA 1992); Matthews v. Circuit Court, 515 So.2d 1065 (Fla. 5th DCA 1987); *See also*, Berens v. Cobb, 539 So.2d 24 (Fla. 2nd DCA 1989) [mandamus was proper remedy where judge refused to rule on a motion].

In Matthews v. Circuit Court, 515 So.2d 1065 (Fla. 5th DCA 1987), the petitioner filed a Rule 3.850 Motion for Postconviction Relief with the trial court on June 26, 1986. The petitioner made repeated requests for a ruling on his 3.850 but received no such ruling. Id. No ruling was issued by the trial court for seventeen months. Id. The district court noted that the trial court had a legal duty to rule on the 3.850. Id. Since the trial court failed to issue a ruling on the 3.850, as was its duty, the district court found that there was no other adequate remedy for the petitioner and granted a writ of mandamus. Id. Said writ ordered the circuit court to promptly rule on the petitioner's 3.850 Motion. Id.

The instant case is similar to Matthews. [***PETITIONER***] filed a 3.850 motion. After waiting ___ months for a ruling from the trial court, [***PETITIONER***] finally filed a motion with said court asking the court to rule on his 3.850 motion. To date, no such order has been issued by the trial court. It is respectfully submitted that there has been more than a reasonable period of time for the trial court to review and rule on [***PETITIONER's***] 3.850. As such, it is submitted that the trial court has not complied with its ministerial duty to rule on [***PETITIONER's***] 3.850 motion within a reasonable period of time.

[***PETITIONER***] has asked the trial court to issue an order on his 3.850 and the trial court has taken no action on said request. It has now been ___ months since [***PETITIONER's***] filed his Motion asking the court to enter an Order on [***PETITIONER's***] 3.850. The trial court has a legal duty to issue an Order on [***PETITIONER's***] 3.850. Despite [***PETITIONER's***] request, the trial court is not acting in accordance with its duty to rule on [***PETITIONER's***] 3.850 within a reasonable time. As such, the trial court has left [***PETITIONER***] with no adequate remedy other than to request a Writ of Mandamus from this Honorable Court. Consequently, [***PETITIONER***] respectfully suggests that, pursuant to Matthews v. Circuit Court, 515 So.2d 1065 (Fla. 5th DCA 1987), this Court should issue a Writ of Mandamus to the Honorable [***Circuit Judge***] of the lower tribunal directing said court to promptly issue a ruling on [***PETITIONER's***] 3.850 Motion for Post Conviction Relief.

WHEREFORE, [***PETITIONER***] respectfully requests that this Honorable Court issue a Writ of Mandamus directing the lower court to promptly rule on [***PETITIONER's***] 3.850 motion.

_(signature line)________________
[***Name, DC#, Address***]

CERTIFICATE OF SERVICE

I HEREBY CERTIFY that a true copy of the foregoing has been furnished by regular U.S. Mail, this [***date***], to the Office of the Attorney General, [***Attorney General's address***].

_(signature line)________________
[***Name***]

FORM 22 – MOTION FOR PERMISSION TO CONDUCT LIMITED DISCOVERY ON MOTION FOR POSTCONVICTION RELIEF

IN THE CIRCUIT COURT OF THE ________ JUDICIAL CIRCUIT,
IN AND FOR ____________ COUNTY, FLORIDA

[***DEFENDANT***],

v. Case No.:_____________

STATE OF FLORIDA.
_____________________/

MOTION FOR PERMISSION TO CONDUCT LIMITED DISCOVERY
ON MOTION FOR POSTCONVICTION RELIEF

[***DEFENDANT***] hereby files this Motion for Permission to Conduct Limited Discovery on Motion for Postconviction Relief, and states:

1. [***DEFENDANT***] currently has pending a Rule 3.850 Motion for Postconviction Relief in the above-captioned case.

2. On [***date***] this Honorable Court entered an order granting an evidentiary hearing on [***DEFENDANT's***] pending 3.850 motion.

3. [***Summarize the issues to be presented at the evidentiary hearing and explain why discovery is necessary for appropriate consideration of said issues***].

4. In postconviction cases, on a motion which sets forth good reason, the court may allow limited discovery into matters which are relevant and material, and where the discovery is permitted, the court may place limitations on the sources and scope. State v. Lewis, 656 So.2d 1248, 1250 (Fla. 1994).

WHEREFORE, [***DEFENDANT***] respectfully requests that this Honorable Court grant this motion and allow Defendant to [***specify the form of discovery to be allowed***].

_(signature line)_______________
[***Name, DC#, Address***]

CERTIFICATE OF SERVICE

I HEREBY CERTIFY that a true copy of the foregoing has been furnished by regular U.S. Mail, this [***date***], to the Office of the State Attorney, [***State Attorney's address***].

_(signature line)________________
[***Name***]

FORM 23 – MOTION TO CORRECT ILLEGAL SENTENCE

IN THE CIRCUIT COURT OF THE ________ JUDICIAL CIRCUIT,
IN AND FOR ____________ COUNTY, FLORIDA

[***DEFENDANT***],

v. Case No.:_____________

STATE OF FLORIDA.
____________________/

RULE 3.800 MOTION TO CORRECT ILLEGAL SENTENCE

[***DEFENDANT***], pursuant to Florida Rule of Criminal Procedure 3.800 hereby files Motion to Correct Illegal Sentence, and states:

1. [***DEFENDANT***] was charged by information in the instant case with [***list charges***].

2. On [***date***], [***DEFENDANT***] was convicted of: _____________.

3. [***DEFENDANT***] was sentences as follows:________________.

4. [***DEFENDANT***] respectfully asserts that his sentence is illegal because [***specify argument and supporting case law to demonstrate illegality of sentence***].

WHEREFORE, [***DEFENDANT***] respectfully moves this court to vacate [***DEFENDANT's***] sentences and [***specify further appropriate relief***].

_(signature line)_______________
[***Name, DC#, Address***]

CERTIFICATE OF SERVICE

I HEREBY CERTIFY that a true copy of the foregoing has been furnished by regular U.S. Mail, this [***date***], to the Office of the State Attorney, [***State Attorney's address***].

_(signature line)_______________
[***Name***]

FORM 24 – MOTION TO DISQUALIFY JUDGE

IN THE CIRCUIT COURT OF THE ________ JUDICIAL CIRCUIT,
IN AND FOR ___________ COUNTY, FLORIDA

[***DEFENDANT***],

v. Case No.:____________

STATE OF FLORIDA.
____________________/

MOTION REQUESTING RECUSAL OF
JUDGE [***JUDGE'S NAME***]

[***DEFENDANT***], pursuant to Florida Judicial Administration Rule 2.330 and Florida Statutes §38.10, respectfully moves for the disqualification of the Honorable [***JUDGE'S NAME***], Circuit Judge, in the above-styled and numbered cause, and states:

1. On or about [***date***], [***DEFENDANT***] filed a Florida Rule of Criminal Procedure 3.850 Motion for Postconviction Relief with this Honorable Court.

2. The Honorable [***JUDGE'S NAME***] is the judge assigned to the above-captioned case.

3. Judicial disqualification is governed by three bodies of law: the Florida Rules of Judicial Administration 2.160 (procedural); Florida Statute §38.10 (statutory); and the Florida Code of Judicial Conduct, Canon 3E(1) (ethical requirements).

4. Florida Rule of Judicial Administration 2.330(b) permits any party to move to disqualify a circuit judge pursuant to any of the aforementioned methods. The procedure for disqualification mandated by this rule begins with a requirement that the movant "allege specifically the facts and reasons" for the disqualification. Fla. R. Jud. Admin., Rule 2.330(c)(2). The facts alleged must pertain to one of the enumerated grounds in Rule 2.330(d). The applicable ground in the case at hand is "the party fears that he or she will not receive a fair trial or hearing because of specifically described prejudice or bias of the judge." Rule 2.330(d)(1); *see also* MacKenzie v. Super Kids Bargain Stores, Inc., 565 So.2d 1332, 1334 (Fla. 1990) (the Florida Supreme Court held that the "facts alleged in [a motion to disqualify] need only show a well-grounded fear that the movant will not receive a fair trial at the hands of the judge."). Once filed, the court "shall determine **only** the legal sufficiency

of the motion." Fla. R. Jud. Admin., Rule 2.330(f) (*emphasis added*). In so doing, the First District Court of Appeal has noted that in determining whether the allegations supporting disqualification are sufficient, the facts must be taken as true and must be viewed from the movant's perspective. Smith v. Santa Rosa Island Authority, 729 So.2d 944 (Fla. 1st DCA 1998). If legally sufficient, the court must grant the motion and take no other action. Fla. R. Jud. Admin. 2.330(f).

5. The Florida Code of Judicial Conduct provides guidance for determining when a motion is "legally sufficient." Pursuant to Canon 3E(1), a judge "shall disqualify himself or herself in a proceeding in which the judge's impartiality might reasonably be questioned." The Florida Supreme Court has held that impartiality "is not a question of how the judge feels," but simply refers to whether the movant possesses a well-grounded fear of judicial partiality. Livingston v. State, 441 So.2d 1083, 1086 (Fla. 1983) ["The question of disqualification focuses on those matters from which a litigant may reasonably question a judge's impartiality rather than the judge's perception of his ability to act fairly and impartially."].

6. While a judge's perceived prejudice is obviously a delicate question, courts have consistently held that so long as the fear is objectively reasonable, disqualification is required. Jarp v. Jarp, 919 So.2d 614 (Fla. 3d DCA 2006); Scott v. State, 909 So.2d 364 (Fla. 5th DCA 2005); Valdes-Fauli v. Valdes-Fauli, 903 So.2d 214 (Fla. 3d DCA 2005). Recusal should occur even when the grounds are supported by only a mere modicum of reason. Livingston, 441 So.2d at 1085. Consequently, a movant need not satisfy numerous strictly applied technical requirements, but must merely demonstrate that, "[i]f taken as a whole, the suggestion and supporting affidavits are sufficient to warrant fear on the part of a party that he will not receive a fair trial by the assigned judge. Id. at 1086.

7. The appropriate standard is whether there is a "well-grounded fear on the part of the movant that he will not receive a fair hearing." Arbelaez v. State, 898 So.2d 25, 41 (Fla. 2005). Such belief must be objectively reasonable. Fischer v. Knuck, 497 So.2d 240, 242 (Fla. 1986). The truthfulness of the allegations must be assumed, and from that point a determination must be made as to whether a reasonably prudent person would be put in fear of not receiving a fair and impartial hearing. Arbelaez, 989 So.2d 41.

8. [***Explain with specificity all facts that demonstrate the bias of the judge***].

9. In light of the above, it is readily apparent that disqualification is necessary. [***The facts demonstrating judicial bias***] create the objectively reasonable fear in [***DEFENDANT***] that he will not receive judicial impartiality in the

present proceedings. When an allegation is raised which questions the judge's neutrality as to one of the parties, the judge can only pass on the legal sufficiency of the allegation; if it is legally sufficient, the trial judge must grant the motion and proceed no further. Smith v. Santa Rosa Island Authority, 729 So.2d 944 (Fla. 1st DCA 1998)

10. It is thus respectfully submitted that the facts presented herein do reasonably give [***DEFENDANT***] a well-grounded fear that he will not receive a fair disposition of his 3.850 motion currently before [***JUDGE'S NAME***].

WHEREFORE, [***DEFENDANT***] respectfully requests that this Honorable Court enter an Order disqualifying [***JUDGE'S NAME***] in this matter for the above-stated reasons.

_(signature line)_______________
[***Name, DC#, Address***]

CERTIFICATE OF SERVICE

I HEREBY CERTIFY that a true copy of the foregoing has been furnished by regular U.S. Mail, this [***date***], to the Office of the State Attorney, [***State Attorney's address***].

_(signature line)_______________
[***Name***]

FORM 25 – PETITION FOR WRIT OF PROHIBITION

IN THE DISTRICT COURT OF APPEAL,
__________ DISTRICT

[***PETITIONER***],
Petitioner,
v. Case No.:_____________

STATE OF FLORIDA,
Respondent.
____________________/

PETITION FOR WRIT OF PROHIBITION

[***PETITIONER***], by and through undersigned counsel, and pursuant to Florida Rule of Appellate Procedure 9.100, respectfully petitions this Court for a writ of prohibition restraining the Honorable [***JUDGE'S NAME***] from presiding as a circuit judge in ________ County Circuit Court case number _________, and states:

I.
BASIS FOR INVOKING JURISDICTION

This Honorable Court has jurisdiction to issue a writ of prohibition under Article V, §4(b)(3) of the Florida Constitution, and Florida Rule of Appellate Procedure 9.030(b)(3). Prohibition is the proper remedy to test the validity of the denial of a motion for disqualification of a judge. *See*, Wal-mart Stores v. Carter, 768 So.2d 21 (Fla. 1st DCA 2000); Rollins v. Baker, 683 So.2d 1138 (Fla. 5th DCA 1996); and, State v. Shaw, 643 So.2d 1163 (Fla. 4th DCA 1994).

II.
NATURE OF THE RELIEF SOUGHT

The nature of the relief sought by this petition is a writ of prohibition directing [***JUDGE***] to grant the Petitioner's Motion for Recusal of [[***JUDGE***] , and restraining [***JUDGE***] from further service as the presiding circuit court judge in [***PETITIONER's***] case.

III.
FACTS UPON WHICH THE PETITIONER RELIES

1. [***Explain with specificity all facts that demonstrate the bias of the judge***].

2. On [***date***], [***PETITIONER***] filed a Motion Requesting Recusal of [***JUDGE***] with the ___ Judicial Circuit Court, in and for ________ County, Florida.

3. On [***date***], [***JUDGE***] issued an Order Denying Motion for Recusal. The Order specified that [***PETITIONER's***] Motion for Recusal was denied because it was legally insufficient. The instant petition follows.

IV.
ARGUMENT

MacKenzie v. Super Kids Bargain Stores, Inc., 565 So.2d 1332 (Fla. 1990) sets out the test for ruling on a motion for disqualification of a judge. In MacKenzie, the Florida Supreme Court held that the "facts alleged in [a motion to disqualify] need only show a well-grounded fear that the movant will not receive a fair trial at the hands of the judge." Id. At 1334; *See also*, Cane v. State, 660 So.2d 705 (Fla. 1995). The First DCA, in reference to MacKenzie, has noted that in determining whether the allegations supporting disqualification are sufficient, the facts must be taken as true and must be viewed from the movant's perspective. Smith v. Santa Rosa Island Authority, 729 So.2d 944 (Fla. 1st DCA 1998). Moreover, whenever an allegation is raised which questions the judge's neutrality as to one of the parties, the judge can only pass on the legal sufficiency of the allegation; if it is legally sufficient, the trial judge must grant the motion and proceed no further. Id.

Based upon the foregoing facts and authorities, it is respectfully submitted that [***PETITIONER***] has a well-founded fear that he will not receive a fair disposition of his currently pending [***type of motion***] from [***JUDGE***]. [***PETITIONER's***] well-founded fear is based upon, but not limited to, the following factors: [***list all factors demonstrating well founded fear of judicial bias***].

It is thus respectfully submitted that the facts presented in [***PETITIONER's***] Motion for Recusal of [***JUDGE***] , and herein, do reasonably give [***PETITIONER***] a well-founded fear that he will not receive a fair disposition of his [***type of motion***] at the hands of [***JUDGE***] .

WHEREFORE, for all of the foregoing reasons, and for good cause shown,

[***PETITIONER***] respectfully requests that this Honorable Court issue a writ of prohibition directing the Honorable [***JUDGE***] to immediately disqualify himself from [***PETITIONER's***] case and restraining [***JUDGE***] from further presiding as a circuit judge in [***PETITIONER's***] case.

_(signature line)________________
[***Name, DC#, Address***]

CERTIFICATE OF SERVICE

I HEREBY CERTIFY that a true copy of the foregoing has been furnished by regular U.S. Mail, this [***date***], to: the Office of the State Attorney, [***State Attorney's address***]; and, [***Judge's name and address***].

_(signature line)________________
[***Name***]

FORM 26 – PUBLIC RECORDS REQUEST

[*date*]

[***Governmental Agency***]
Custodian of Records
[***Address***]

Re: Public Records Request
State v. ____________
________ County Circuit Case #____________

To Whom it May Concern:

This is a request for public records maintained by your office and is made pursuant to Section 119.01, et.seq., Florida Statutes. I hereby request a copy of the following described records, in the above-referenced case, which are maintained by or in the possession of the [***Governmental Agency***], to wit: [***specify all records required or ask for full copy of file***].

As required by §119.07(1)(d)-(f), Florida Statutes, if you claim that any of the records which are the subject of this request are exempt from the provisions of §119.07, Florida Statutes, you are requested to: (a) produce in a timely manner the remainder of those records requested herein which have become public and for which no exemption is claimed; and, (b) state the basis of the exemption(s) which you contend is/are applicable, including the statutory citation to such exemption created or afforded by statute, and to state in writing, with particularity, the reason for your conclusion that the record(s) is/are exempt.

Thank you in advance for your anticipated cooperation and attention to this matter. Please let me know the cost of the copies and I will promptly remit a check in said amount. Please do not hesitate to contact me if you have any questions or concerns regarding my request.

_(signature line)_______________
[***Name, DC#, Address***]

APPENDIX A – TITLE 28 U.S.C. §2254 FORM

Petition for Relief From a Conviction or Sentence
By a Person in State Custody

(Petition Under 28 U.S.C. § 2254 for a Writ of Habeas Corpus)

Instructions

1. To use this form, you must be a person who is currently serving a sentence under a judgment against you in a state court. You are asking for relief from the conviction or the sentence. This form is your petition for relief.

2. You may also use this form to challenge a state judgment that imposed a sentence to be served in the future, but you must fill in the name of the state where the judgment was entered. If you want to challenge a federal judgment that imposed a sentence to be served in the future, you should file a motion under 28 U.S.C. § 2255 in the federal court that entered the judgment.

3. Make sure the form is typed or neatly written.

4. You must tell the truth and sign the form. If you make a false statement of a material fact, you may be prosecuted for perjury.

5. Answer all the questions. You do not need to cite law. You may submit additional pages if necessary. If you do not fill out the form properly, you will be asked to submit additional or correct information. If you want to submit a brief or arguments, you must submit them in a separate memorandum.

6. You must pay a fee of $5. If the fee is paid, your petition will be filed. If you cannot pay the fee, you may ask to proceed in forma pauperis (as a poor person). To do that, you must fill out the last page of this form. Also, you must submit a certificate signed by an officer at the institution where you are confined showing the amount of money that the institution is holding for you. If your account exceeds $ ________ , you must pay the filing fee.

7. In this petition, you may challenge the judgment entered by only one court. If you want to challenge a judgment entered by a different court (either in the same state or in different states), you must file a separate petition.

8. When you have completed the form, send the original and ____ copies to the Clerk of the United States District Court at this address:

   Clerk, United States District Court for
   Address
   City, State Zip Code

   If you want a file-stamped copy of the petition, you must enclose an additional copy of the petition and ask the court to file-stamp it and return it to you.

9. **<u>CAUTION:</u> You must include in this petition all the grounds for relief from the conviction or sentence that you challenge. And you must state the facts that support each ground. If you fail to set forth all the grounds in this petition, you may be barred from presenting additional grounds at a later date.**

10. **<u>CAPITAL CASES:</u> If you are under a sentence of death, you are entitled to the assistance of counsel and should request the appointment of counsel.**

PETITION UNDER 28 U.S.C. § 2254 FOR WRIT OF HABEAS CORPUS BY A PERSON IN STATE CUSTODY

United States District Court	District:
Name (under which you were convicted):	Docket or Case No.:
Place of Confinement :	Prisoner No.:
Petitioner (include the name under which you were convicted) v.	Respondent (authorized person having custody of petitioner)
The Attorney General of the State of:	

PETITION

1. (a) Name and location of court that entered the judgment of conviction you are challenging:

   (b) Criminal docket or case number (if you know):

2. (a) Date of the judgment of conviction (if you know):

   (b) Date of sentencing:

3. Length of sentence:

4. In this case, were you convicted on more than one count or of more than one crime? ❐ Yes ❐ No

5. Identify all crimes of which you were convicted and sentenced in this case:

6. (a) What was your plea? (Check one)

   ❐ (1) Not guilty ❐ (3) Nolo contendere (no contest)

   ❐ (2) Guilty ❐ (4) Insanity plea

(b) If you entered a guilty plea to one count or charge and a not guilty plea to another count or charge, what did you plead guilty to and what did you plead not guilty to? ______

(c) If you went to trial, what kind of trial did you have? (Check one)

❒ Jury ❒ Judge only

7. Did you testify at a pretrial hearing, trial, or a post-trial hearing?

❒ Yes ❒ No

8. Did you appeal from the judgment of conviction?

❒ Yes ❒ No

9. If you did appeal, answer the following:

(a) Name of court: ______

(b) Docket or case number (if you know): ______

(c) Result: ______

(d) Date of result (if you know): ______

(e) Citation to the case (if you know): ______

(f) Grounds raised: ______

(g) Did you seek further review by a higher state court? ❒ Yes ❒ No

If yes, answer the following:

(1) Name of court: ______

(2) Docket or case number (if you know): ______

(3) Result: ______

(4) Date of result (if you know): ______

(5) Citation to the case (if you know): ____________________

(6) Grounds raised: ____________________

(h) Did you file a petition for certiorari in the United States Supreme Court? ❐ Yes ❐ No

If yes, answer the following:

(1) Docket or case number (if you know): ____________________

(2) Result: ____________________

(3) Date of result (if you know): ____________________

(4) Citation to the case (if you know): ____________________

10. Other than the direct appeals listed above, have you previously filed any other petitions, applications, or motions concerning this judgment of conviction in any state court? ❐ Yes ❐ No

11. If your answer to Question 10 was "Yes," give the following information:

(a) (1) Name of court: ____________________

(2) Docket or case number (if you know): ____________________

(3) Date of filing (if you know): ____________________

(4) Nature of the proceeding: ____________________

(5) Grounds raised: ____________________

(6) Did you receive a hearing where evidence was given on your petition, application, or motion?

❐ Yes ❐ No

(7) Result: ____________________

(8) Date of result (if you know): ____________________

(b) If you filed any second petition, application, or motion, give the same information:

(1) Name of court: ______

(2) Docket or case number (if you know): ______

(3) Date of filing (if you know): ______

(4) Nature of the proceeding: ______

(5) Grounds raised: ______

(6) Did you receive a hearing where evidence was given on your petition, application, or motion?

❒ Yes ❒ No

(7) Result: ______

(8) Date of result (if you know): ______

(c) If you filed any third petition, application, or motion, give the same information:

(1) Name of court: ______

(2) Docket or case number (if you know): ______

(3) Date of filing (if you know): ______

(4) Nature of the proceeding: ______

(5) Grounds raised: ______

(6) Did you receive a hearing where evidence was given on your petition, application, or motion?

❒ Yes ❒ No

(7) Result: ______________________________

(8) Date of result (if you know): ______________________________

(d) Did you appeal to the highest state court having jurisdiction over the action taken on your petition, application, or motion?

(1) First petition: ❒ Yes ❒ No

(2) Second petition: ❒ Yes ❒ No

(3) Third petition: ❒ Yes ❒ No

(e) If you did not appeal to the highest state court having jurisdiction, explain why you did not:

12. For this petition, state every ground on which you claim that you are being held in violation of the Constitution, laws, or treaties of the United States. Attach additional pages if you have more than four grounds. State the facts supporting each ground.

CAUTION: To proceed in the federal court, you must ordinarily first exhaust (use up) your available state-court remedies on each ground on which you request action by the federal court. Also, if you fail to set forth all the grounds in this petition, you may be barred from presenting additional grounds at a later date.

GROUND ONE: ______________________________

(a) Supporting facts (Do not argue or cite law. Just state the specific facts that support your claim.):

(b) If you did not exhaust your state remedies on Ground One, explain why: ______________________________

(c) **Direct Appeal of Ground One:**

(1) If you appealed from the judgment of conviction, did you raise this issue? ❐ Yes ❐ No

(2) If you did not raise this issue in your direct appeal, explain why:

(d) **Post-Conviction Proceedings:**

(1) Did you raise this issue through a post-conviction motion or petition for habeas corpus in a state trial court?

❐ Yes ❐ No

(2) If your answer to Question (d)(1) is "Yes," state:

Type of motion or petition:

Name and location of the court where the motion or petition was filed:

Docket or case number (if you know):

Date of the court's decision:

Result (attach a copy of the court's opinion or order, if available):

(3) Did you receive a hearing on your motion or petition? ❐ Yes ❐ No

(4) Did you appeal from the denial of your motion or petition? ❐ Yes ❐ No

(5) If your answer to Question (d)(4) is "Yes," did you raise this issue in the appeal? ❐ Yes ❐ No

(6) If your answer to Question (d)(4) is "Yes," state:

Name and location of the court where the appeal was filed:

Docket or case number (if you know):

Date of the court's decision:

Result (attach a copy of the court's opinion or order, if available):

(7) If your answer to Question (d)(4) or Question (d)(5) is "No," explain why you did not raise this issue:

(e) **Other Remedies:** Describe any other procedures (such as habeas corpus, administrative remedies, etc.) that you have used to exhaust your state remedies on Ground One:

GROUND TWO:

(a) Supporting facts (Do not argue or cite law. Just state the specific facts that support your claim.):

(b) If you did not exhaust your state remedies on Ground Two, explain why:

(c) **Direct Appeal of Ground Two:**

(1) If you appealed from the judgment of conviction, did you raise this issue? ❒ Yes ❒ No

(2) If you did not raise this issue in your direct appeal, explain why:

(d) **Post-Conviction Proceedings:**

(1) Did you raise this issue through a post-conviction motion or petition for habeas corpus in a state trial court?

❒ Yes ❒ No

(2) If your answer to Question (d)(1) is "Yes," state:

Type of motion or petition:

Name and location of the court where the motion or petition was filed:

Docket or case number (if you know):

Date of the court's decision:

Result (attach a copy of the court's opinion or order, if available):

(3) Did you receive a hearing on your motion or petition? ❒ Yes ❒ No

(4) Did you appeal from the denial of your motion or petition? ❒ Yes ❒ No

(5) If your answer to Question (d)(4) is "Yes," did you raise this issue in the appeal? ❒ Yes ❒ No

(6) If your answer to Question (d)(4) is "Yes," state:

Name and location of the court where the appeal was filed:

Docket or case number (if you know):

Date of the court's decision:

Result (attach a copy of the court's opinion or order, if available):

(7) If your answer to Question (d)(4) or Question (d)(5) is "No," explain why you did not raise this issue:

(e) **Other Remedies:** Describe any other procedures (such as habeas corpus, administrative remedies, etc.) that you have used to exhaust your state remedies on Ground Two :

GROUND THREE:

(a) Supporting facts (Do not argue or cite law. Just state the specific facts that support your claim.):

(b) If you did not exhaust your state remedies on Ground Three, explain why: ______________________

(c) **Direct Appeal of Ground Three:**

(1) If you appealed from the judgment of conviction, did you raise this issue? ❒ Yes ❒ No

(2) If you did not raise this issue in your direct appeal, explain why: ______________________

(d) **Post-Conviction Proceedings:**

(1) Did you raise this issue through a post-conviction motion or petition for habeas corpus in a state trial court?

❒ Yes ❒ No

(2) If your answer to Question (d)(1) is "Yes," state:

Type of motion or petition: ______________________

Name and location of the court where the motion or petition was filed: ______________________

Docket or case number (if you know): ______________________

Date of the court's decision: ______________________

Result (attach a copy of the court's opinion or order, if available): ______________________

(3) Did you receive a hearing on your motion or petition? ❒ Yes ❒ No

(4) Did you appeal from the denial of your motion or petition? ❒ Yes ❒ No

(5) If your answer to Question (d)(4) is "Yes," did you raise this issue in the appeal? ❒ Yes ❒ No

(6) If your answer to Question (d)(4) is "Yes," state:

Name and location of the court where the appeal was filed: ______________________

Docket or case number (if you know): ______________________

Date of the court's decision: ______________________

Result (attach a copy of the court's opinion or order, if available): ______________________

(7) If your answer to Question (d)(4) or Question (d)(5) is "No," explain why you did not raise this issue:

(e) **Other Remedies:** Describe any other procedures (such as habeas corpus, administrative remedies, etc.) that you have used to exhaust your state remedies on Ground Three:

GROUND FOUR:

(a) Supporting facts (Do not argue or cite law. Just state the specific facts that support your claim.):

(b) If you did not exhaust your state remedies on Ground Four, explain why:

(c) **Direct Appeal of Ground Four:**

(1) If you appealed from the judgment of conviction, did you raise this issue? ❒ Yes ❒ No

(2) If you did not raise this issue in your direct appeal, explain why:

(d) **Post-Conviction Proceedings**:

(1) Did you raise this issue through a post-conviction motion or petition for habeas corpus in a state trial court?

❒ Yes ❒ No

(2) If your answer to Question (d)(1) is "Yes," state:

Type of motion or petition:

Name and location of the court where the motion or petition was filed: ______________________

____

Docket or case number (if you know): ______________________

Date of the court's decision: ______________________

Result (attach a copy of the court's opinion or order, if available): ______________________

____

____

(3) Did you receive a hearing on your motion or petition? ❐ Yes ❐ No

(4) Did you appeal from the denial of your motion or petition? ❐ Yes ❐ No

(5) If your answer to Question (d)(4) is "Yes," did you raise this issue in the appeal? ❐ Yes ❐ No

(6) If your answer to Question (d)(4) is "Yes," state:

Name and location of the court where the appeal was filed: ______________________

____

Docket or case number (if you know): ______________________

Date of the court's decision: ______________________

Result (attach a copy of the court's opinion or order, if available): ______________________

____

____

____

(7) If your answer to Question (d)(4) or Question (d)(5) is "No," explain why you did not raise this issue:

____

____

____

____

____

____

(e) **Other Remedies:** Describe any other procedures (such as habeas corpus, administrative remedies, etc.) that you have used to exhaust your state remedies on Ground Four: ______________________

____

____

____

____

____

____

13. Please answer these additional questions about the petition you are filing:

(a) Have all grounds for relief that you have raised in this petition been presented to the highest state court having jurisdiction? ❒ Yes ❒ No

If your answer is "No," state which grounds have not been so presented and give your reason(s) for not presenting them: ______________________________

(b) Is there any ground in this petition that has not been presented in some state or federal court? If so, which ground or grounds have not been presented, and state your reasons for not presenting them:

____

14. Have you previously filed any type of petition, application, or motion in a federal court regarding the conviction that you challenge in this petition? ❒ Yes ❒ No

If "Yes," state the name and location of the court, the docket or case number, the type of proceeding, the issues raised, the date of the court's decision, and the result for each petition, application, or motion filed. Attach a copy of any court opinion or order, if available. ______________________________

15. Do you have any petition or appeal now pending (filed and not decided yet) in any court, either state or federal, for the judgment you are challenging? ❒ Yes ❒ No

If "Yes," state the name and location of the court, the docket or case number, the type of proceeding, and the issues raised. ______________________________

16. Give the name and address, if you know, of each attorney who represented you in the following stages of the judgment you are challenging:

(a) At preliminary hearing: ______

(b) At arraignment and plea: ______

(c) At trial: ______

(d) At sentencing: ______

(e) On appeal: ______

(f) In any post-conviction proceeding: ______

(g) On appeal from any ruling against you in a post-conviction proceeding: ______

17. Do you have any future sentence to serve after you complete the sentence for the judgment that you are challenging? ❒ Yes ❒ No

(a) If so, give name and location of court that imposed the other sentence you will serve in the future:

(b) Give the date the other sentence was imposed: ______

(c) Give the length of the other sentence: ______

(d) Have you filed, or do you plan to file, any petition that challenges the judgment or sentence to be served in the future? ❒ Yes ❒ No

18. TIMELINESS OF PETITION: If your judgment of conviction became final over one year ago, you must explain why the one-year statute of limitations as contained in 28 U.S.C. § 2244(d) does not bar your petition.*

* The Antiterrorism and Effective Death Penalty Act of 1996 ("AEDPA") as contained in 28 U.S.C. § 2244(d) provides in part that:

(1) A one-year period of limitation shall apply to an application for a writ of habeas corpus by a person in custody pursuant to the judgment of a State court. The limitation period shall run from the latest of -

(A) the date on which the judgment became final by the conclusion of direct review or the expiration of the time for seeking such review;

(B) the date on which the impediment to filing an application created by State action in violation of the Constitution or laws of the United States is removed, if the applicant was prevented from filing by such state action;

(C) the date on which the constitutional right asserted was initially recognized by the Supreme Court, if the right has been newly recognized by the Supreme Court and made retroactively applicable to cases on collateral review; or

(D) the date on which the factual predicate of the claim or claims presented could have been discovered through the exercise of due diligence.

(2) The time during which a properly filed application for State post-conviction or other collateral review with respect to the pertinent judgment or claim is pending shall not be counted toward any period of limitation under this subsection.

Therefore, petitioner asks that the Court grant the following relief: ______________________________

____

____

or any other relief to which petitioner may be entitled.

____

Signature of Attorney (if any)

I declare (or certify, verify, or state) under penalty of perjury that the foregoing is true and correct and that this Petition for Writ of Habeas Corpus was placed in the prison mailing system on ______________ (month, date, year).

Executed (signed) on ______________ (date).

____

Signature of Petitioner

If the person signing is not petitioner, state relationship to petitioner and explain why petitioner is not signing this petition.

____

____

____

____

APPENDIX B – TITLE 28 U.S.C. §2255 FORM

Motion to Vacate, Set Aside, or Correct a Sentence By a Person in Federal Custody

(Motion Under 28 U.S.C. § 2255)

Instructions

1. To use this form, you must be a person who is serving a sentence under a judgment against you in a federal court. You are asking for relief from the conviction or the sentence. This form is your motion for relief.
2. You must file the form in the United States district court that entered the judgment that you are challenging. If you want to challenge a federal judgment that imposed a sentence to be served in the future, you should file the motion in the federal court that entered that judgment.
3. Make sure the form is typed or neatly written.
4. You must tell the truth and sign the form. If you make a false statement of a material fact, you may be prosecuted for perjury.
5. Answer all the questions. You do not need to cite law. You may submit additional pages if necessary. If you do not fill out the form properly, you will be asked to submit additional or correct information. If you want to submit a brief or arguments, you must submit them in a separate memorandum.
6. If you cannot pay for the costs of this motion (such as costs for an attorney or transcripts), you may ask to proceed *in forma pauperis* (as a poor person). To do that, you must fill out the last page of this form. Also, you must submit a certificate signed by an officer at the institution where you are confined showing the amount of money that the institution is holding for you.
7. In this motion, you may challenge the judgment entered by only one court. If you want to challenge a judgment entered by a different judge or division (either in the same district or in a different district), you must file a separate motion.
8. When you have completed the form, send the original and ____ copies to the Clerk of the United States District Court at this address:

   Clerk, United States District Court for
   Address
   City, State Zip Code

   If you want a file-stamped copy of the petition, you must enclose an additional copy of the petition and ask the court to file-stamp it and return it to you.
9. **CAUTION: You must include in this motion all the grounds for relief from the conviction or sentence that you challenge. And you must state the facts that support each ground. If you fail to set forth all the grounds in this motion, you may be barred from presenting additional grounds at a later date.**
10. **CAPITAL CASES: If you are under a sentence of death, you are entitled to the assistance of counsel and should request the appointment of counsel.**

MOTION UNDER 28 U.S.C. § 2255 TO VACATE, SET ASIDE, OR CORRECT

SENTENCE BY A PERSON IN FEDERAL CUSTODY

United States District Court	District	
Name *(under which you were convicted)*:		Docket or Case No.:
Place of Confinement:	Prisoner No.:	
UNITED STATES OF AMERICA	V.	Movant *(include name under which convicted)*

MOTION

1. (a) Name and location of court which entered the judgment of conviction you are challenging:

   (b) Criminal docket or case number (if you know): ______

2. (a) Date of the judgment of conviction (if you know): ______

   (b) Date of sentencing: ______

3. Length of sentence: ______

4. Nature of crime (all counts):

5. (a) What was your plea? (Check one)
   (1) Not guilty ☐ (2) Guilty ☐ (3) Nolo contendere (no contest) ☐

   (b) If you entered a guilty plea to one count or indictment, and a not guilty plea to another count or what did you plead guilty to and what did you plead not guilty to?

6. If you went to trial, what kind of trial did you have? (Check one) Jury ☐ Judge only ☐

7. Did you testify at a pretrial hearing, trial, or post-trial hearing? Yes ☐ No ☐

8. Did you appeal from the judgment of conviction? Yes ☐ No ☐

9. If you did appeal, answer the following:

(a) Name of court: ____________________

(b) Docket or case number (if you know): ____________________

(c) Result: ____________________

(d) Date of result (if you know): ____________________

(e) Citation to the case (if you know): ____________________

(f) Grounds raised:

____

(g) Did you file a petition for certiorari in the United States Supreme Court? Yes ☐ No ☐

If "Yes," answer the following:

(1) Docket or case number (if you know): ____________________

(2) Result: ____________________

____

(3) Date of result (if you know): ____________________

(4) Citation to the case (if you know): ____________________

(5) Grounds raised:

____

10. Other than the direct appeals listed above, have you previously filed any other motions, petitions, or applications, concerning this judgment of conviction in any court?

Yes ☐ No ☐

11. If your answer to Question 10 was "Yes," give the following information:

(a) (1) Name of court: ____________________

(2) Docket or case number (if you know): ____________________

(3) Date of filing (if you know): ____________________

(4) Nature of the proceeding: ____________________

(5) Grounds raised: ____________________

____

(6) Did you receive a hearing where evidence was given on your motion, petition, or application?

Yes ☐ No ☐

(7) Result: ______

(8) Date of result (if you know): ______

(b) If you filed any second motion, petition, or application, give the same information:

(1) Name of court: ______

(2) Docket of case number (if you know): ______

(3) Date of filing (if you know): ______

(4) Nature of the proceeding: ______

(5) Grounds raised:

______

(6) Did you receive a hearing where evidence was given on your motion, petition, or application?

Yes ☐ No ☐

(7) Result: ______

(8) Date of result (if you know): ______

(c) Did you appeal to a federal appellate court having jurisdiction over the action taken on your motion, petition, or application?

(1) First petition: Yes ☐ No ☐

(2) Second petition: Yes ☐ No ☐

(d) If you did not appeal from the action on any motion, petition, or application, explain briefly why you did not:

______

12. For this motion, state every ground on which you claim that you are being held in violation of the Constitution, laws, or treaties of the United States. Attach additional pages if you have more than four grounds. State the facts supporting each ground.

GROUND ONE: ____________________

(a) Supporting facts (Do not argue or cite law. Just state the specific facts that support your claim.):

(b) **Direct Appeal of Ground One:**

(1) If you appealed from the judgment of conviction, did you raise this issue?

Yes ☐ No ☐

(2) If you did not raise this issue in your direct appeal, explain why:

(c) **Post-Conviction Proceedings:**

(1) Did you raise this issue in any post-conviction motion, petition, or application?

Yes ☐ No ☐

(2) If you answer to Question (c)(1) is "Yes," state:

Type of motion or petition: ____________________

Name and location of the court where the motion or petition was filed:

Docket or case number (if you know): ____________________

Date of the court's decision: ____________________

Result (attach a copy of the court's opinion or order, if available):

(3) Did you receive a hearing on your motion, petition, or application?

Yes ☐ No ☐

(4) Did you appeal from the denial of your motion, petition, or application?

Yes ☐ No ☐

(5) If your answer to Question (c)(4) is "Yes," did you raise the issue in the appeal?

Yes ☐ No ☐

(6) If your answer to Question (c)(4) is "Yes," state:

Name and location of the court where the appeal was filed:

Docket or case number (if you know):

Date of the court's decision:

Result (attach a copy of the court's opinion or order, if available):

(7) If your answer to Question (c)(4) or Question (c)(5) is "No," explain why you did not appeal or raise this issue:

GROUND TWO:

(a) Supporting facts (Do not argue or cite law. Just state the specific facts that support your claim.):

(b) **Direct Appeal of Ground Two:**

(1) If you appealed from the judgment of conviction, did you raise this issue?

Yes ☐ No ☐

(2) If you did not raise this issue in your direct appeal, explain why:

(c) **Post-Conviction Proceedings:**

(1) Did you raise this issue in any post-conviction motion, petition, or application?

Yes ☐ No ☐

(2) If you answer to Question (c)(1) is "Yes," state:

Type of motion or petition: ______

Name and location of the court where the motion or petition was filed:

______

Docket or case number (if you know): ______

Date of the court's decision: ______

Result (attach a copy of the court's opinion or order, if available):

______

(3) Did you receive a hearing on your motion, petition, or application?

Yes ☐ No ☐

(4) Did you appeal from the denial of your motion, petition, or application?

Yes ☐ No ☐

(5) If your answer to Question (c)(4) is "Yes," did you raise the issue in the appeal?

Yes ☐ No ☐

(6) If your answer to Question (c)(4) is "Yes," state:

Name and location of the court where the appeal was filed:

______

Docket or case number (if you know): ______

Date of the court's decision: ______

Result (attach a copy of the court's opinion or order, if available):

______

(7) If your answer to Question (c)(4) or Question (c)(5) is "No," explain why you did not appeal or raise this issue:

______

GROUND THREE: ______

______

(a) Supporting facts (Do not argue or cite law. Just state the specific facts that support your claim.):

______

(b) **Direct Appeal of Ground Three:**

(1) If you appealed from the judgment of conviction, did you raise this issue?

Yes ☐ No ☐

(2) If you did not raise this issue in your direct appeal, explain why:

(c) **Post-Conviction Proceedings:**

(1) Did you raise this issue in any post-conviction motion, petition, or application?

Yes ☐ No ☐

(2) If you answer to Question (c)(1) is "Yes," state:

Type of motion or petition:

Name and location of the court where the motion or petition was filed:

Docket or case number (if you know):

Date of the court's decision:

Result (attach a copy of the court's opinion or order, if available):

(3) Did you receive a hearing on your motion, petition, or application?

Yes ☐ No ☐

(4) Did you appeal from the denial of your motion, petition, or application?

Yes ☐ No ☐

(5) If your answer to Question (c)(4) is "Yes," did you raise the issue in the appeal?

Yes ☐ No ☐

(6) If your answer to Question (c)(4) is "Yes," state:

Name and location of the court where the appeal was filed:

Docket or case number (if you know):

Date of the court's decision:

Result (attach a copy of the court's opinion or order, if available):

(7) If your answer to Question (c)(4) or Question (c)(5) is "No," explain why you did not appeal or raise this issue:

GROUND FOUR:

(a) Supporting facts (Do not argue or cite law. Just state the specific facts that support your claim.):

(b) **Direct Appeal of Ground Four:**

(1) If you appealed from the judgment of conviction, did you raise this issue?

Yes ☐ No ☐

(2) If you did not raise this issue in your direct appeal, explain why:

(c) **Post-Conviction Proceedings:**

(1) Did you raise this issue in any post-conviction motion, petition, or application?

Yes ☐ No ☐

(2) If you answer to Question (c)(1) is "Yes," state:

Type of motion or petition:

Name and location of the court where the motion or petition was filed:

Docket or case number (if you know):

Date of the court's decision:

Result (attach a copy of the court's opinion or order, if available):

(3) Did you receive a hearing on your motion, petition, or application?

Yes ☐ No ☐

(4) Did you appeal from the denial of your motion, petition, or application?

Yes ☐ No ☐

(5) If your answer to Question (c)(4) is "Yes," did you raise the issue in the appeal?

Yes ☐ No ☐

(6) If your answer to Question (c)(4) is "Yes," state:

Name and location of the court where the appeal was filed:

Docket or case number (if you know):

Date of the court's decision:

Result (attach a copy of the court's opinion or order, if available):

(7) If your answer to Question (c)(4) or Question (c)(5) is "No," explain why you did not appeal or raise this issue:

13. Is there any ground in this motion that you have not previously presented in some federal court? If so, which ground or grounds have not been presented, and state your reasons for not presenting them:

14. Do you have any motion, petition, or appeal now pending (filed and not decided yet) in any court for the you are challenging? Yes ☐ No ☐

If "Yes," state the name and location of the court, the docket or case number, the type of proceeding, and the issues raised.

15. Give the name and address, if known, of each attorney who represented you in the following stages of the you are challenging:
   (a) At the preliminary hearing:

   (b) At the arraignment and plea:

   (c) At the trial:

   (d) At sentencing:

   (e) On appeal:

   (f) In any post-conviction proceeding:

   (g) On appeal from any ruling against you in a post-conviction proceeding:

16. Were you sentenced on more than one court of an indictment, or on more than one indictment, in the same court and at the same time? Yes ☐ No ☐

17. Do you have any future sentence to serve after you complete the sentence for the judgment that you are challenging? Yes ☐ No ☐
   (a) If so, give name and location of court that imposed the other sentence you will serve in the future:

   (b) Give the date the other sentence was imposed:
   (c) Give the length of the other sentence:
   (d) Have you filed, or do you plan to file, any motion, petition, or application that challenges the judgment or sentence to be served in the future? Yes ☐ No ☐

18. TIMELINESS OF MOTION: If your judgment of conviction became final over one year ago, you must explain why the one-year statute of limitations as contained in 28 U.S.C. § 2255 does not bar your motion.*

* The Antiterrorism and Effective Death Penalty Act of 1996 ("AEDPA") as contained in 28 U.S.C. § 2255, paragraph 6, provides in part that:

A one-year period of limitation shall apply to a motion under this section. The limitation period shall run from the latest of –

(1) the date on which the judgment of conviction became final;

(2) the date on which the impediment to making a motion created by governmental action in violation of the Constitution or laws of the United States is removed, if the movant was prevented from making such a motion by such governmental action;

(3) the date on which the right asserted was initially recognized by the Supreme Court, if that right has been newly recognized by the Supreme Court and made retroactively applicable to cases on collateral review; or

(4) the date on which the facts supporting the claim or claims presented could have been discovered through the exercise of due diligence.

Therefore, movant asks that the Court grant the following relief:

____

or any other relief to which movant may be entitled.

____
Signature of Attorney (if any)

I declare (or certify, verify, or state) under penalty of perjury that the foregoing is true and correct and that this Motion under 28 U.S.C. § 2255 was placed in the prison mailing system on _______________________.
(month, date, year)

Executed (signed) on _______________________ (date)

____
Signature of Movant

If the person signing is not movant, state relationship to movant and explain why movant is not signing this motion.

APPENDIX C – SELECTED FLORIDA RULES OF CRIMINAL PROCEDURE

Rule 3.800. Correction, Reduction, and Modification of Sentences

(a) Correction.

(1) *Generally.* A court may at any time correct an illegal sentence imposed by it, or an incorrect calculation made by it in a sentencing scoresheet, when it is affirmatively alleged that the court records demonstrate on their face an entitlement to that relief, provided that a party may not file a motion to correct an illegal sentence under this subdivision during the time allowed for the filing of a motion under subdivision (b)(1) or during the pendency of a direct appeal.

(2) *Successive Motions.* A court may dismiss a second or successive motion if the court finds that the motion fails to allege new or different grounds for relief and the prior determination was on the merits. When a motion is dismissed under this subdivision, a copy of that portion of the files and records necessary to support the court's ruling must accompany the order dismissing the motion.

(3) *Sexual Predator Designation.* A defendant may seek correction of an allegedly erroneous sexual predator designation under this subdivision, but only when it is apparent from the face of the record that the defendant did not meet the criteria for designation as a sexual predator.

(4) *Appeals.* All orders denying or dismissing motions under subdivision (a) must include a statement that the defendant has the right to appeal within 30 days of rendition of the order.

(b) Motion to Correct Sentencing Error. A motion to correct any sentencing error, including an illegal sentence, may be filed as allowed by this subdivision. This subdivision shall not be applicable to those cases in which the death sentence has been imposed and direct appeal jurisdiction is in the Supreme Court under article V, section 3(b)(1) of the Florida Constitution. The motion must identify the error with specificity and provide a proposed correction. A response to the motion may be filed within 15 days, either admitting or contesting the alleged error. Motions may be filed by the state under this subdivision only if the correction of the sentencing error would benefit the defendant or to correct a scrivener's error.

(1) *Motion Before Appeal.* During the time allowed for the filing of a notice of appeal of a sentence, a defendant or the state may file a motion to correct a sentencing error.

(A) This motion shall stay rendition under Florida Rule of Appellate Procedure 9.020(i).

(B) Unless the trial court determines that the motion can be resolved as a matter of law without a hearing, it shall hold a calendar call no later than 20 days from the filing of the motion, with notice to all parties, for the express purpose of either ruling on the motion or determining the need for an evidentiary hearing. If an evidentiary hearing is needed, it shall be set no more than 20 days from the date of the calendar call. Within 60 days from the filing of the motion, the trial court shall file an order ruling on the motion. A party may file a motion for rehearing of any signed, written order entered under subdivisions (a) and (b) of this rule within 15 days of the date of service of the order or within 15 days of the expiration of the time period for filing an order if no order is filed. A response may be filed within 10 days of service of the motion. The trial court's order disposing of the motion for rehearing shall be filed within 15 days of the response but not later than 40 days from the date of the order of which rehearing is sought. A timely filed motion for rehearing shall toll rendition of the order subject to appellate review and the order shall be deemed rendered upon the filing of a signed, written order denying the motion for rehearing.

(2) *Motion Pending Appeal.* If an appeal is pending, a defendant or the state may file in the trial court a motion to correct a sentencing error. The motion may be filed by appellate counsel and must be served before the party's first brief is served. A notice of pending motion to correct sentencing error shall be filed in the appellate court, which notice automatically shall extend the time for the filing of the brief until 10 days after the clerk of circuit court transmits the supplemental record under Florida Rule of Appellate Procedure 9.140(f)(6).

(A) The motion shall be served on the trial court and on all trial and appellate counsel of record. Unless the motion expressly states that appellate counsel will represent the movant in the trial court, trial counsel will represent the movant on the motion under Florida Rule of Appellate Procedure 9.140(d). If the state is the movant, trial counsel will represent the defendant unless appellate counsel for the defendant notifies trial counsel and the trial court that he or she will represent the defendant on the state's motion.

(B) The trial court shall resolve this motion in accordance with the procedures in subdivision (b)(1)(B), except that if the trial court does not file an order ruling on the motion within 60 days, the motion shall be deemed denied. Similarly, if the trial court does not file an order ruling on a timely motion for rehearing within 40 days from the date of the order of which rehearing is sought, the motion for rehearing shall be deemed denied.

(C) In accordance with Florida Rule of Appellate Procedure 9.140(f)(6), the clerk of circuit court shall supplement the appellate record with the motion, the order, any amended sentence, and, if designated, a transcript of any additional portion of the proceedings.

(c) Reduction and Modification. A court may reduce or modify to include any of the provisions of chapter 948, Florida Statutes, a legal sentence imposed by it, sua sponte, or upon motion filed, within 60 days after the imposition, or within 60 days after receipt by the court of a mandate issued by the appellate court on affirmance of the judgment and/or sentence on an original appeal, or within 60 days after receipt by the court of a certified copy of an order of the appellate court dismissing an original appeal from the judgment and/or sentence, or, if further appellate review is sought in a higher court or in successively higher courts, within 60 days after the highest state or federal court to which a timely appeal has been taken under authority of law, or in which a petition for certiorari has been timely filed under authority of law, has entered an order of affirmance or an order dismissing the appeal and/or denying certiorari. If review is upon motion, the trial court shall have 90 days from the date the motion is filed or such time as agreed by the parties or as extended by the trial court to enter an order ruling on the motion. This subdivision shall not be applicable to those cases in which the death sentence is imposed or those cases in which the trial judge has imposed the minimum mandatory sentence or has no sentencing discretion.

Rule 3.801. Correction of Jail Credit

(a) Correction of Jail Credit. A court may correct a sentence that fails to allow a defendant credit for all of the time he or she spent in the county jail before sentencing as provided in section 921.161, Florida Statutes.

(b) Time Limitations. No motion shall be filed or considered pursuant to this rule if filed more than 1 year after the sentence becomes final. For sentences imposed prior to July 1, 2013, a motion under this rule may be filed on or before July 1, 2014.

(c) Contents of Motion. The motion shall be under oath and include:

(1) a brief statement of the facts relied on in support of the motion;

(2) the dates, location of incarceration and total time for credit already provided;

(3) the dates, location of incarceration and total time for credit the defendant contends was not properly awarded;

(4) whether any other criminal charges were pending at the time of the incarceration noted in subdivision (c)(3), and if so, the location, case number and resolution of the charges; and

(5) whether the defendant waived any county jail credit at the time of sentencing, and if so, the number of days waived.

(d) Successive Motions. No successive motions for jail credit will be considered.

(e) Incorporation of Portions of Florida Rule of Criminal Procedure 3. 850. The following subdivisions of Florida Rule of Criminal Procedure 3.850 apply to proceedings under this rule: 3.850(e), (f), (j), (k), and (n).

Rule 3.850. Motion to Vacate, Set Aside, or Correct Sentence

(a) Grounds for Motion. The following grounds may be claims for relief from judgment or release from custody by a person who has been tried and found guilty or has entered a plea of guilty or nolo contendere before a court established by the laws of Florida:

(1) The judgment was entered or sentence was imposed in violation of the Constitution or laws of the United States or the State of Florida.

(2) The court did not have jurisdiction to enter the judgment.

(3) The court did not have jurisdiction to impose the sentence.

(4) The sentence exceeded the maximum authorized by law.

(5) The plea was involuntary.

(6) The judgment or sentence is otherwise subject to collateral attack.

(b) Time Limitations. A motion to vacate a sentence that exceeds the limits provided by law may be filed at any time. No other motion shall be filed or considered pursuant to this rule if filed more than 2 years after the judgment and sentence become final unless it alleges that

(1) the facts on which the claim is predicated were unknown to the movant or the movant's attorney and could not have been ascertained by the exercise of due diligence, and the claim is made within 2 years of the time the new facts were or could have been discovered with the exercise of due diligence, or

(2) the fundamental constitutional right asserted was not established within the period provided for herein and has been held to apply retroactively, and the claim is made within 2 years of the date of the mandate of the decision announcing the retroactivity, or

(3) the defendant retained counsel to timely file a 3.850 motion and counsel, through neglect, failed to file the motion. A claim based on this exception shall not be filed more than 2 years after the expiration of the time for filing a motion for postconviction relief.

(c) Contents of Motion. The motion must be under oath stating that the defendant has read the motion or that it has been read to him or her, that the defendant understands its content, and that all of the facts stated therein are true and correct. The motion must also include an explanation of:

(1) the judgment or sentence under attack and the court that rendered the same;

(2) whether the judgment resulted from a plea or a trial;

(3) whether there was an appeal from the judgment or sentence and the disposition thereof;

(4) whether a previous postconviction motion has been filed, and if so, how many;

(5) if a previous motion or motions have been filed, the reason or reasons the claim or claims in the present motion were not raised in the former motion or motions;

(6) the nature of the relief sought; and

(7) a brief statement of the facts and other conditions relied on in support of the motion.

This rule does not authorize relief based on grounds that could have or should have been raised at trial and, if properly preserved, on direct appeal of the judgment and sentence. If the defendant is filing a newly discovered evidence claim based on recanted trial testimony or on a newly discovered witness, the defendant shall include an affidavit from that person as an attachment to his or her motion. For all other newly discovered evidence claims, the defendant shall attach an affidavit from any person whose testimony is necessary to factually support the defendant's claim for relief. If the affidavit is not attached to the motion, the defendant shall provide an explanation why the required affidavit could not be obtained.

(d) Form of Motion. Motions shall be typewritten or hand-written in legible printed lettering, in blue or black ink, double-spaced, with margins no less than 1 inch on white 8 1/2-by-11 inch paper. No motion, including any memorandum of law, shall exceed 50 pages without leave of the court upon a showing of good cause.

(e) Amendments to Motion. When the court has entered an order under subdivision (f)(2) or (f)(3), granting the defendant an opportunity to amend the motion, any amendment to the motion must be served within 60 days. A motion may otherwise be amended at any time prior to either the entry of an order disposing of the motion or the entry of an order pursuant to subdivision (f)(5) or directing that an answer to the motion be filed pursuant to (f)(6), whichever occurs first. Leave of court is required for the filing of an amendment after the entry of an order pursuant to subdivision (f)(5) or (f)(6). Notwithstanding the timeliness of an amendment, the court need not consider new factual assertions contained in an amendment unless the amendment is under oath. New claims for relief contained in an amendment need not be considered by the court unless the amendment is filed within the time frame specified in subdivision (b).

(f) Procedure; Evidentiary Hearing; Disposition. On filing of a motion under this rule, the clerk shall forward the motion and file to the court. Disposition of the motion shall be in accordance with the following procedures, which are intended to result in a single, final, appealable order that disposes of all claims raised in the motion.

(1) *Untimely and Insufficient Motions.* If the motion is insufficient on its face, and the time to file a motion under this rule has expired prior to the filing of the

motion, the court shall enter a final appealable order summarily denying the motion with prejudice.

(2) *Timely but Insufficient Motions.* If the motion is insufficient on its face, and the motion is timely filed under this rule, the court shall enter a nonfinal, nonappealable order allowing the defendant 60 days to amend the motion. If the amended motion is still insufficient or if the defendant fails to file an amended motion within the time allowed for such amendment, the court, in its discretion, may permit the defendant an additional opportunity to amend the motion or may enter a final, appealable order summarily denying the motion with prejudice.

(3) *Timely Motions Containing Some Insufficient Claims.* If the motion sufficiently states one or more claims for relief and it also attempts but fails to state additional claims, and the motion is timely filed under this rule, the court shall enter a nonappealable order granting the defendant 60 days to amend the motion to sufficiently state additional claims for relief. Any claim for which the insufficiency has not been cured within the time allowed for such amendment shall be summarily denied in an order that is a nonfinal, nonappealable order, which may be reviewed when a final, appealable order is entered.

(4) *Motions Partially Disposed of by the Court Record.* If the motion sufficiently states one or more claims for relief but the files and records in the case conclusively show that the defendant is not entitled to relief as to one or more claims, the claims that are conclusively refuted shall be summarily denied on the merits without a hearing. A copy of that portion of the files and records in the case that conclusively shows that the defendant is not entitled to relief as to one or more claims shall be attached to the order summarily denying these claims. The files and records in the case are the documents and exhibits previously filed in the case and those portions of the other proceedings in the case that can be transcribed. An order that does not resolve all the claims is a nonfinal, nonappealable order, which may be reviewed when a final, appealable order is entered.

(5) *Motions Conclusively Resolved by the Court Record.* If the motion is legally sufficient but all grounds in the motion can be conclusively resolved either as a matter of law or by reliance upon the records in the case, the motion shall be denied without a hearing by the entry of a final order. If the denial is based on the records in the case, a copy of that portion of the files and records that

conclusively shows that the defendant is entitled to no relief shall be attached to the final order.

(6) *Motions Requiring a Response from the State Attorney.* Unless the motion, files, and records in the case conclusively show that the defendant is entitled to no relief, the court shall order the state attorney to file, within the time fixed by the court, an answer to the motion. The answer shall respond to the allegations contained in the defendant's sufficiently pleaded claims, describe any matters in avoidance of the sufficiently pleaded claims, state whether the defendant has used any other available state postconviction remedies including any other motion under this rule, and state whether the defendant has previously been afforded an evidentiary hearing.

(7) *Appointment of Counsel.* The court may appoint counsel to represent the defendant under this rule. The factors to be considered by the court in making this determination include: the adversary nature of the proceeding, the complexity of the proceeding, the complexity of the claims presented, the defendant's apparent level of intelligence and education, the need for an evidentiary hearing, and the need for substantial legal research.

(8) *Disposition by Evidentiary Hearing.*

(A) If an evidentiary hearing is required, the court shall grant a prompt hearing and shall cause notice to be served on the state attorney and the defendant or defendant's counsel, and shall determine the issues, and make findings of fact and conclusions of law with respect thereto.

(B) At an evidentiary hearing, the defendant shall have the burden of presenting evidence and the burden of proof in support of his or her motion, unless otherwise provided by law.

(C) The order issued after the evidentiary hearing shall resolve all the claims raised in the motion and shall be considered the final order for purposes of appeal.

(g) Defendant's Presence Not Required. The defendant's presence shall not be required at any hearing or conference held under this rule except at the evidentiary hearing on the merits of any claim.

(h) Successive Motions.

(1) A second or successive motion must be titled: "Second or Successive Motion for Postconviction Relief."

(2) A second or successive motion is an extraordinary pleading. Accordingly, a court may dismiss a second or successive motion if the court finds that it fails to allege new or different grounds for relief and the prior determination was on the merits or, if new and different grounds are alleged, the judge finds that the failure of the defendant or the attorney to assert those grounds in a prior motion constituted an abuse of the procedure or there was no good cause for the failure of the defendant or defendant's counsel to have asserted those grounds in a prior motion. When a motion is dismissed under this subdivision, a copy of that portion of the files and records necessary to support the court's ruling shall accompany the order denying the motion.

(i) Service on Parties. The clerk of the court shall promptly serve on the parties a copy of any order entered under this rule, noting thereon the date of service by an appropriate certificate of service.

(j) Rehearing. Any party may file a motion for rehearing of any order addressing a motion under this rule within 15 days of the date of service of the order. A motion for rehearing is not required to preserve any issue for review in the appellate court. A motion for rehearing must be based on a good faith belief that the court has overlooked a previously argued issue of fact or law or an argument based on a legal precedent or statute not available prior to the court's ruling. A response may be filed within 10 days of service of the motion. The trial court's order disposing of the motion for rehearing shall be filed within 15 days of the response but not later than 40 days from the date of the order of which rehearing is sought.

(k) Appeals. An appeal may be taken to the appropriate appellate court only from the final order disposing of the motion. All final orders denying motions for postconviction relief shall include a statement that the defendant has the right to appeal within 30 days of the rendition of the order. All nonfinal, nonappealable orders entered pursuant to subdivision (f) should include a statement that the defendant has no right to appeal the order until entry of the final order.

(l) Belated Appeals and Discretionary Review. Pursuant to the procedures outlined in Florida Rule of Appellate Procedure 9.141, a defendant may seek a belated appeal or discretionary review.

(m) Habeas Corpus. An application for writ of habeas corpus on behalf of a prisoner who is authorized to apply for relief by motion pursuant to this rule shall not be entertained if it appears that the applicant has failed to apply for relief, by motion, to the court that sentenced the applicant or that the court has denied the applicant relief, unless it also appears that the remedy by motion is inadequate or ineffective to test the legality of the applicant's detention.

(n) Certification of Defendant; Sanctions. No motion may be filed pursuant to this rule unless it is filed in good faith and with a reasonable belief that it is timely, has potential merit, and does not duplicate previous motions that have been disposed of by the court.

(1) By signing a motion pursuant to this rule, the defendant certifies that: the defendant has read the motion or that it has been read to the defendant and that the defendant understands its content; the motion is filed in good faith and with a reasonable belief that it is timely filed, has potential merit, and does not duplicate previous motions that have been disposed of by the court; and, the facts contained in the motion are true and correct.

(2) The defendant shall either certify that the defendant can understand English or, if the defendant cannot understand English, that the defendant has had the motion translated completely into a language that the defendant understands. The motion shall contain the name and address of the person who translated the motion and that person shall certify that he or she provided an accurate and complete translation to the defendant. Failure to include this information and certification in a motion shall be grounds for the entry of an order dismissing the motion pursuant to subdivision (f)(1), (f)(2), or (f)(3).

(3) Conduct prohibited under this rule includes, but is not limited to, the following: the filing of frivolous or malicious claims; the filing of any motion in bad faith or with reckless disregard for the truth; the filing of an application for habeas corpus subject to dismissal pursuant to subdivision (m); the willful violation of any provision of this rule; and the abuse of the legal process or procedures governed by this rule.

The court, upon its own motion or on the motion of a party, may determine whether a motion has been filed in violation of this rule. The court shall issue an order setting forth the facts indicating that the defendant has or may have engaged in prohibited conduct. The order shall direct the defendant to show cause, within a reasonable time limit set by the court, why the court should not find that the defendant has engaged in prohibited conduct under this rule and impose an appropriate sanction. Following the issuance of the order to show cause and the filing of any response by the defendant, and after such further hearing as the court may deem appropriate, the court shall make a final determination of whether the defendant engaged in prohibited conduct under this subsection.

(4) If the court finds by the greater weight of the evidence that the defendant has engaged in prohibited conduct under this rule, the court may impose one or more sanctions, including:

(A) contempt as otherwise provided by law;

(B) assessing the costs of the proceeding against the defendant;

(C) dismissal with prejudice of the defendant's motion;

(D) prohibiting the filing of further pro se motions under this rule and directing the clerk of court to summarily reject any further pro se motion under this rule;

(E) requiring that any further motions under this rule be signed by a member in good standing of The Florida Bar, who shall certify that there is a good faith basis for each claim asserted in the motion; and/or

(F) if the defendant is a prisoner, a certified copy of the order be forwarded to the appropriate institution or facility for consideration of disciplinary action against the defendant, including forfeiture of gain time pursuant to Chapter 944, Florida Statutes.

(5) If the court determines there is probable cause to believe that a sworn motion contains a false statement of fact constituting perjury, the court may refer the matter to the state attorney.

Rule 3.851. Collateral Relief After Death Sentence has Been Imposed and Affirmed on Direct Appeal

(a) Scope. This rule shall apply to all postconviction proceedings that commence upon issuance of the appellate mandate affirming the death sentence to include all motions and petitions for any type of postconviction or collateral relief brought by a defendant in state custody who has been sentenced to death and whose conviction and death sentence have been affirmed on direct appeal. It shall apply to all postconviction motions filed on or after January 1, 2015, by defendants who are under sentence of death. Motions pending on that date are governed by the version of this rule in effect immediately prior to that date.

(b) Appointment of Postconviction Counsel.

(1) Upon the issuance of the mandate affirming a judgment and sentence of death on direct appeal, the Supreme Court of Florida shall at the same time issue an order appointing the appropriate office of the Capital Collateral Regional Counsel or directing the trial court to immediately appoint counsel from the Registry of Attorneys maintained by the Justice Administrative Commission. The name of Registry Counsel shall be filed with the Supreme Court of Florida.

(2) Within 30 days of the issuance of the mandate, the Capital Collateral Regional Counsel or Registry Counsel shall file either a notice of appearance or a motion to withdraw in the trial court. Motions to withdraw filed more than 30 days after the issuance of the mandate shall not be entertained unless based on a specific conflict of interest as set forth in section 27.703, Florida Statutes.

(3) Within 15 days after Capital Collateral Regional Counsel or Registry Counsel files a motion to withdraw, the chief judge or assigned judge shall rule on the motion and appoint new postconviction counsel if necessary. The appointment of new collateral counsel shall be from the Registry of attorneys maintained by the Justice Administrative Commission unless the case is administratively transferred to another Capital Collateral Regional Counsel.

(4) In every capital postconviction case, one lawyer shall be designated as lead counsel for the defendant. The lead counsel shall be the defendant's primary lawyer in all state court litigation. No lead counsel shall be permitted to appear for a limited purpose on behalf of a defendant in a capital postconviction proceeding.

(5) After the filing of a notice of appearance, Capital Collateral Regional Counsel, Registry Counsel, or a private attorney shall represent the defendant in the state courts until a judge allows withdrawal or until the sentence is reversed, reduced, or carried out, regardless of whether another attorney represents the defendant in a federal court.

(6) A defendant who has been sentenced to death may not represent himself or herself in a capital postconviction proceeding in state court. The only bases for a defendant to seek to dismiss postconviction counsel in state court shall be pursuant to statute due to actual conflict or subdivision (i) of this rule.

(c) Preliminary Procedures.

(1) *Judicial Assignment and Responsibilities.* Within 30 days of the issuance of mandate affirming a judgment and sentence of death on direct appeal, the chief judge shall assign the case to a judge qualified under the Rules of Judicial Administration to conduct capital proceedings. The assigned judge is responsible for case management to ensure compliance with statutes, rules, and administrative orders that impose processing steps, time deadlines, and reporting requirements for capital postconviction litigation. From the time of assignment, the judge must issue case management orders for every step of the capital postconviction process, including at the conclusion of all hearings and conferences.

(2) *Status Conferences.* The assigned judge shall conduct a status conference not later than 90 days after the judicial assignment, and shall hold status conferences at least every 90 days thereafter until the evidentiary hearing has been completed or the motion has been ruled on without a hearing. The attorneys, with leave of the trial court, may appear electronically at the status conferences. Requests to appear electronically shall be liberally granted. Pending motions, disputes involving public records, or any other matters ordered by the court shall be heard at the status conferences.

(3) *Defendant's Presence Not Required.* The defendant's presence shall not be required at any hearing or conference held under this rule, except at the evidentiary hearing on the merits of any claim and at any hearing involving conflict with or removal of collateral counsel.

(4) *Duties of Defense Counsel.* Within 45 days of appointment of postconviction counsel, the defendant's trial counsel shall provide to postconviction counsel a copy of the original file including all work product not otherwise subject to a protective order and information pertaining to the defendant's capital case which was created and obtained during the representation of the defendant. Postconviction counsel shall maintain the confidentiality of all confidential information received. Postconviction counsel shall bear the costs of any copying. The defendant's trial counsel must retain the defendant's original file.

(5) *Record on Direct Appeal.* The Clerk of the Circuit Court shall retain a copy of the record for the direct appeal when the record is transmitted to the Supreme Court of Florida. The Clerk of the Supreme Court of Florida shall deliver the record on appeal to the records repository within 30 days after the appointment of postconviction counsel.

(d) Time Limitation.

(1) Any motion to vacate judgment of conviction and sentence of death shall be filed by the defendant within 1 year after the judgment and sentence become final. For the purposes of this rule, a judgment is final:

(A) on the expiration of the time permitted to file in the United States Supreme Court a petition for writ of certiorari seeking review of the Supreme Court of Florida decision affirming a judgment and sentence of death (90 days after the opinion becomes final); or

(B) on the disposition of the petition for writ of certiorari by the United States Supreme Court, if filed.

(2) No motion shall be filed or considered pursuant to this rule if filed beyond the time limitation provided in subdivision (d)(1) unless it alleges:

(A) the facts on which the claim is predicated were unknown to the movant or the movant's attorney and could not have been ascertained by the exercise of due diligence, or

(B) the fundamental constitutional right asserted was not established within the period provided for in subdivision (d)(1) and has been held to apply retroactively, or

(C) postconviction counsel, through neglect, failed to file the motion.

(3) All petitions for extraordinary relief in which the Supreme Court of Florida has original jurisdiction, including petitions for writs of habeas corpus, shall be filed simultaneously with the initial brief filed on behalf of the death-sentenced defendant in the appeal of the circuit court's order on the initial motion for postconviction relief filed under this rule.

(4) If the governor signs a death warrant before the expiration of the time limitation in subdivision (d)(1), the Supreme Court of Florida, on a defendant's request, will grant a stay of execution to allow any postconviction relief motions to proceed in a timely and orderly manner.

(5) An extension of time may be granted by the Supreme Court of Florida for the filing of postconviction pleadings if the defendant's counsel makes a showing that due to exceptional circumstances, counsel was unable to file the postconviction pleadings within the 1-year period established by this rule.

(e) Contents of Motion.

(1) *Initial Motion.* A motion filed under this rule is an initial postconviction motion if no state court has previously ruled on a postconviction motion challenging the same judgment and sentence. An initial motion and memorandum of law filed under this rule shall not exceed 75 pages exclusive of the attachments. Each claim or subclaim shall be separately pled and shall be sequentially numbered beginning with claim number 1. If upon motion or upon the court's own motion, a judge determines that this portion of the rule has not been followed, the judge shall give the movant 30 days to amend. If no amended motion is filed, the judge shall deem the non-compliant claim, subclaim, and/or argument waived. Attachments shall include, but are not limited to, the judgment and sentence. The memorandum of law shall set forth the applicable case law supporting the granting of relief as to each separately pled claim. This rule does not authorize relief based upon claims that could have or should have been raised at trial and, if properly preserved, on direct appeal of the judgment and sentence. If claims that were raised on appeal or should have or could have been raised on appeal are contained in the motion, the memorandum of law shall contain a brief statement explaining why these claims are being raised on postconviction relief. The motion need not be under oath or signed by the defendant but shall include:

(A) a description of the judgment and sentence under attack and the court that rendered the same;

(B) a statement of each issue raised on appeal and the disposition thereof;

(C) the nature of the relief sought;

(D) a detailed allegation of the factual basis for any claim for which an evidentiary hearing is sought;

(E) a detailed allegation as to the basis for any purely legal or constitutional claim for which an evidentiary hearing is not required and the reason that this claim could not have been or was not raised on direct appeal; and

(F) a certification from the attorney that he or she has discussed the contents of the motion fully with the defendant, that he or she has complied with Rule 4-1.4 of the Rules of Professional Conduct, and that the motion is filed in good faith.

(2) *Successive Motion.* A motion filed under this rule is successive if a state court has previously ruled on a postconviction motion challenging the same judgment and sentence. A claim raised in a successive motion shall be dismissed if the trial

court finds that it fails to allege new or different grounds for relief and the prior determination was on the merits; or, if new and different grounds are alleged, the trial court finds that the failure to assert those grounds in a prior motion constituted an abuse of the procedure; or, if the trial court finds there was no good cause for failing to assert those grounds in a prior motion; or, if the trial court finds the claim fails to meet the time limitation exceptions set forth in subdivision (d)(2)(A), (d)(2)(B), or (d)(2)(C). A successive motion shall not exceed 25 pages, exclusive of attachments, and shall include:

(A) all of the pleading requirements of an initial motion under subdivision (e)(1);

(B) the disposition of all previous claims raised in postconviction proceedings and the reason or reasons the claim or claims raised in the present motion were not raised in the former motion or motions;

(C) if based upon newly discovered evidence, *Brady v. Maryland*, 373 U.S. 83 (1963), or *Giglio v. United States*, 405 U.S. 150 (1972), the following:

(i) the names, addresses, and telephone numbers of all witnesses supporting the claim;

(ii) a statement that the witness will be available, should an evidentiary hearing be scheduled, to testify under oath to the facts alleged in the motion or affidavit;

(iii) if evidentiary support is in the form of documents, copies of all documents shall be attached, including any affidavits obtained; and

(iv) as to any witness or document listed in the motion or attachment to the motion, a statement of the reason why the witness or document was not previously available.

(f) Procedure; Evidentiary Hearing; Disposition.

(1) *Filing and Service.* All pleadings in the postconviction proceeding shall be filed with the clerk of the trial court and served on the assigned judge, opposing party, and the attorney general. Upon the filing of any original court document in the postconviction proceeding, the clerk of the trial court shall determine that the assigned judge has received a copy. All motions other than the postconviction motion itself shall be accompanied by a notice of hearing.

(2) *Duty of Clerk.* A motion filed under this rule shall be immediately delivered to the chief judge or the assigned judge along with the court file.

(3) *Answer.*

(A) Answer to the Initial Motion. Within 60 days of the filing of an initial motion, the state shall file its answer. The answer and accompanying memorandum of law shall not exceed 75 pages, exclusive of attachments and exhibits. The answer shall address the legal insufficiency of any claim in the motion, respond to the allegations of the motion, and address any procedural bars. The answer shall use the same claim numbering system contained in the defendant's initial motion. As to any claims of legal insufficiency or procedural bar, the state shall include a short statement of any applicable case law.

(B) Answer to a Successive Motion. Within 20 days of the filing of a successive motion, the state shall file its answer. The answer shall not exceed 25 pages, exclusive of attachments and exhibits. The answer shall use the same claim numbering system contained in the defendant's motion. The answer shall specifically respond to each claim in the motion and state the reason(s) that an evidentiary hearing is or is not required.

(4) *Amendments.* A motion filed under this rule may not be amended unless good cause is shown. A copy of the claim sought to be added must be attached to the motion to amend. The trial court may in its discretion grant a motion to amend provided that the motion to amend was filed at least 45 days before the scheduled evidentiary hearing. Granting a motion under this subdivision shall not be a basis for granting a continuance of the evidentiary hearing unless a manifest injustice would occur if a continuance was not granted. If amendment is allowed, the state shall file an amended answer within 20 days after the judge allows the motion to be amended.

(5) *Case Management Conference; Evidentiary Hearing.*

(A) Initial Postconviction Motion. No later than 90 days after the state files its answer to an initial motion, the trial court shall hold a case management conference. At the case management conference, the defendant shall disclose all documentary exhibits that he or she intends to offer at the evidentiary hearing and shall file and serve an exhibit list of all such exhibits and a witness list with the names and addresses of any potential witnesses. All expert witnesses shall be specifically designated on the witness list and copies of all expert reports shall be attached. Within 60 days after the case management conference, the state shall disclose all documentary exhibits that it intends to offer at the evidentiary hearing and shall file and serve an exhibit list of all such exhibits and a witness list with the names and addresses of any potential witnesses. All expert witnesses shall be specifically designated on the witness list and copies of all expert reports shall be attached. At the case management conference, the trial court shall:

(i) schedule an evidentiary hearing, to be held within 150 days, on claims listed by the defendant as requiring a factual determination;

(ii) hear argument on any purely legal claims not based on disputed facts; and

(iii) resolve disputes arising from the exchange of information under this subdivision.

(B) Successive Postconviction Motion. Within 30 days after the state files its answer to a successive motion for postconviction relief, the trial court shall hold a case management conference. At the case management conference, the trial court also shall determine whether an evidentiary hearing should be held and hear argument on any purely legal claims not based on disputed facts. If the motion, files, and records in the case conclusively show that the movant is entitled to no relief, the motion may be denied without an evidentiary hearing. If the trial court determines that an evidentiary hearing should be held, the court shall schedule the hearing to be held within 90 days. If a death warrant has been signed, the trial court shall expedite these time periods in accordance with subdivision (h) of this rule.

(C) Extension of Time to Hold Evidentiary Hearing. The trial court also may for good cause extend the time for holding an evidentiary hearing for up to 90 days.

(D) Taking Testimony. Upon motion, or upon its own motion and without the consent of any party, the court may permit a witness to testify at the evidentiary hearing by contemporaneous video communication equipment that makes the witness visible to all parties during the testimony. There must be appropriate safeguards for the court to maintain sufficient control over the equipment and the transmission of the testimony so the court may stop the communication to accommodate objections or prevent prejudice. If testimony is taken through video communication equipment, there must be a notary public or other person authorized to administer oaths in the witness's jurisdiction who is present with the witness and who administers the oath consistent with the laws of the jurisdiction where the witness is located. The cost for the use of video communication equipment is the responsibility of either the requesting party or, if upon its own motion, the court.

(E) Procedures After Evidentiary Hearing. Immediately following an evidentiary hearing, the trial court shall order a transcript of the hearing, which shall be filed within 10 days if real-time transcription was utilized, or within 45 days if real-time transcription was not utilized. The trial judge may permit written closing arguments instead of oral closing arguments. If the trial court permits the parties to submit written closing arguments, the arguments shall be filed by both parties within 30 days of the filing of the transcript of the hearing. No answer or reply arguments shall be allowed. Written arguments shall be in compliance with the requirements for briefs in rule 9.210(a)(1) and (a)(2), shall not exceed 60 pages without leave of court, and shall include proposed findings of facts and conclusions of law, with citations to authority and to appropriate portions of the transcript of the hearing.

(F) Rendition of the Order. If the court does not permit written closing arguments, the court shall render its order within 30 days of the filing of the transcript of the hearing. If the court permits written closing arguments, the court shall render its order within 30 days of the filing of the last written closing argument and no later than 60 days from the filing of the transcript of the hearing. The court shall rule on each claim considered at the evidentiary hearing and all other claims raised in the motion, making detailed findings of fact and conclusions of law with respect to each claim, and attaching or referencing such portions of the record as are necessary to allow for meaningful appellate review. The order issued after the evidentiary hearing shall resolve all the claims raised in the motion and shall be considered the final order for purposes of appeal. The clerk of the trial court shall promptly serve upon the parties and the attorney general a copy of the final order, with a certificate of service.

(6) *Experts and Other Witnesses.* All expert witnesses who will testify at the evidentiary hearing must submit written reports, which shall be disclosed to opposing counsel as provided in subdivision (f)(5)(A). If the defendant intends to offer expert testimony of his or her mental status, the state shall be entitled to have the defendant examined by its own mental health expert. If the defendant fails to cooperate with the state's expert, the trial court may, in its discretion, proceed as provided in rule 3.202(e).

(7) *Rehearing.* Motions for rehearing shall be filed within 15 days of the rendition of the trial court's order and a response thereto filed within 10 days

thereafter. A motion for rehearing shall be based on a good faith belief that the court has overlooked a previously argued issue of fact or law or an argument based on a legal precedent or statute not available prior to the court's ruling. The trial court's order disposing of the motion for rehearing shall be rendered not later than 30 days from the filing of the motion for rehearing. If no order is filed within 30 days from the filing of the motion for rehearing, the motion is deemed denied. A motion for rehearing is not required to preserve any issue for review.

(8) *Appeals.* Any party may appeal a final order entered on a defendant's motion for rule 3.851 relief by filing a notice of appeal with the clerk of the lower tribunal within 30 days of the rendition of the order to be reviewed. Pursuant to the procedures outlined in Florida Rule of Appellate Procedure 9.142, a defendant under sentence of death may petition for a belated appeal.

(g) Incompetence to Proceed in Capital Collateral Proceedings.

(1) A death-sentenced defendant pursuing collateral relief under this rule who is found by the court to be mentally incompetent shall not be proceeded against if there are factual matters at issue, the development or resolution of which require the defendant's input. However, all collateral relief issues that involve only matters of record and claims that do not require the defendant's input shall proceed in collateral proceedings notwithstanding the defendant's incompetency.

(2) Collateral counsel may file a motion for competency determination and an accompanying certificate of counsel that the motion is made in good faith and on reasonable grounds to believe that the death-sentenced defendant is incompetent to proceed.

(3) If, at any stage of a postconviction proceeding, the court determines that there are reasonable grounds to believe that a death-sentenced defendant is incompetent to proceed and that factual matters are at issue, the development or resolution of which require the defendant's input, a judicial determination of incompetency is required.

(4) The motion for competency examination shall be in writing and shall allege with specificity the factual matters at issue and the reason that competent consultation with the defendant is necessary with respect to each factual matter specified. To the extent that it does not invade the lawyer-client privilege with collateral counsel, the motion shall contain a recital of the specific observations

of, and conversations with, the death-sentenced defendant that have formed the basis of the motion.

(5) If the court finds that there are reasonable grounds to believe that a death-sentenced defendant is incompetent to proceed in a postconviction proceeding in which factual matters are at issue, the development or resolution of which require the defendant's input, the court shall order the defendant examined by no more than 3, nor fewer than 2, experts before setting the matter for a hearing. The court may seek input from the death-sentenced defendant's counsel and the state attorney before appointment of the experts.

(6) The order appointing experts shall:

(A) identify the purpose of the evaluation and specify the area of inquiry that should be addressed;

(B) specify the legal criteria to be applied; and

(C) specify the date by which the report shall be submitted and to whom it shall be submitted.

(7) Counsel for both the death-sentenced defendant and the state may be present at the examination, which shall be conducted at a date and time convenient for all parties and the Department of Corrections.

(8) On appointment by the court, the experts shall examine the death-sentenced defendant with respect to the issue of competence to proceed, as specified by the court in its order appointing the experts to evaluate the defendant, and shall evaluate the defendant as ordered.

(A) The experts first shall consider factors related to the issue of whether the death-sentenced defendant meets the criteria for competence to proceed, that is, whether the defendant has sufficient present ability to consult with counsel with a reasonable degree of rational understanding and whether the defendant has a rational as well as factual understanding of the pending collateral proceedings.

(B) In considering the issue of competence to proceed, the experts shall consider and include in their report:

(i) the defendant's capacity to understand the adversary nature of the legal process and the collateral proceedings;

(ii) the defendant's ability to disclose to collateral counsel facts pertinent to the postconviction proceeding at issue; and

(iii) any other factors considered relevant by the experts and the court as specified in the order appointing the experts.

(C) Any written report submitted by an expert shall:

(i) identify the specific matters referred for evaluation;

(ii) describe the evaluative procedures, techniques, and tests used in the examination and the purpose or purposes for each;

(iii) state the expert's clinical observations, findings, and opinions on each issue referred by the court for evaluation, and indicate specifically those issues, if any, on which the expert could not give an opinion; and

(iv) identify the sources of information used by the expert and present the factual basis for the expert's clinical findings and opinions.

(9) If the experts find that the death-sentenced defendant is incompetent to proceed, the experts shall report on any recommended treatment for the defendant to attain competence to proceed. In considering the issues relating to treatment, the experts shall report on:

(A) the mental illness or intellectual disability causing the incompetence;

(B) the treatment or treatments appropriate for the mental illness or intellectual disability of the defendant and an explanation of each of the possible treatment alternatives in order of choices; and

(C) the likelihood of the defendant attaining competence under the treatment recommended, an assessment of the probable duration of the treatment required to restore competence, and the probability that the defendant will attain competence to proceed in the foreseeable future.

(10) Within 30 days after the experts have completed their examinations of the death-sentenced defendant, the court shall schedule a hearing on the issue of the defendant's competence to proceed.

(11) If, after a hearing, the court finds the defendant competent to proceed, or, after having found the defendant incompetent, finds that competency has been restored, the court shall enter its order so finding and shall proceed with a postconviction motion. The defendant shall have 60 days to amend his or her rule 3.851 motion only as to those issues that the court found required factual consultation with counsel.

(12) If the court docs not find the defendant incompetent, the order shall contain:

(A) findings of fact relating to the issues of competency;

(B) copies of the reports of the examining experts; and

(C) copies of any other psychiatric, psychological, or social work reports submitted to the court relative to the mental state of the death-sentenced defendant.

(13) If the court finds the defendant incompetent or finds the defendant competent subject to the continuation of appropriate treatment, the court shall follow the procedures set forth in rule 3.212(c), except that, to the extent practicable, any treatment shall take place at a custodial facility under the direct supervision of the Department of Corrections.

(h) After Death Warrant Signed.

(1) *Judicial Assignment.* The chief judge of the circuit shall assign the case to a judge qualified under the Rules of Judicial Administration to conduct capital cases as soon as notification of the death warrant is received.

(2) *Calendar Advancement.* Proceedings after a death warrant has been issued shall take precedence over all other cases. The assigned judge shall make every effort to resolve scheduling conflicts with other cases including cancellation or rescheduling of hearings or trials and requesting senior judge assistance.

(3) *Schedule of Proceedings.* The time limitations in this rule shall not apply after a death warrant has been signed. All motions shall be heard expeditiously considering the time limitations set by the date of execution and the time required for appellate review.

(4) *Location of Hearings.* The location of hearings after a death warrant is signed shall be determined by the trial judge considering the availability of witnesses or evidence, the security problems involved in the case, and any other factor determined by the trial court.

(5) *Postconviction Motions.* All motions filed after a death warrant is issued shall be considered successive motions and subject to the content requirement of subdivision (e)(2) of this rule.

(6) *Case Management Conference.* The assigned judge shall schedule a case management conference as soon as reasonably possible after receiving notification that a death warrant has been signed. During the case management conference the court shall set a time for filing a postconviction motion and shall schedule a hearing to determine whether an evidentiary hearing should be held and hear argument on any purely legal claims not based on disputed facts. If the motion, files, and records in the case conclusively show that the movant is entitled to no relief, the motion may be denied without an evidentiary hearing. If

the trial court determines that an evidentiary hearing should be held, the court shall schedule the hearing to be held as soon as reasonably possible considering the time limitations set by the date of execution and the time required for appellate review.

(7) *Reporting*. The assigned judge shall require the proceedings conducted under death warrant to be reported using the most advanced and accurate technology available in general use at the location of the hearing. The proceedings shall be transcribed expeditiously considering the time limitations set by the execution date.

(8) *Procedures After Hearing*. The court shall obtain a transcript of all proceedings and shall render its order as soon as possible after the hearing is concluded. A copy of the final order shall be electronically transmitted to the Supreme Court of Florida and to the attorneys of record.

(9) *Transmittal of Record*. The record shall be immediately delivered to the clerk of the Supreme Court of Florida by the clerk of the trial court or as ordered by the assigned judge. The record shall also be electronically transmitted if the technology is available. A notice of appeal shall not be required to transmit the record.

(i) Dismissal of Postconviction Proceedings.

(1) This subdivision applies only when a defendant seeks both to dismiss pending postconviction proceedings and to discharge collateral counsel.

(2) If the defendant files the motion pro se, the Clerk of the Court shall serve copies of the motion on counsel of record for both the defendant and the state. Counsel of record may file responses within 10 days.

(3) The trial judge shall review the motion and the responses and schedule a hearing. The defendant, collateral counsel, and the state shall be present at the hearing.

(4) The judge shall examine the defendant at the hearing and shall hear argument of the defendant, collateral counsel, and the state. No fewer than 2 or more than 3 qualified experts shall be appointed to examine the defendant if the judge concludes that there are reasonable grounds to believe the defendant is not mentally competent for purposes of this rule. The experts shall file reports with the court setting forth their findings. Thereafter, the court shall conduct an evidentiary hearing and enter an order setting forth findings of competency or incompetency.

(5) If the defendant is found to be incompetent for purposes of this rule, the court shall deny the motion without prejudice.

(6) If the defendant is found to be competent for purposes of this rule, the court shall conduct a complete (*Durocher/Faretta*) inquiry to determine whether the defendant knowingly, freely and voluntarily wants to dismiss pending postconviction proceedings and discharge collateral counsel.

(7) If the court determines that the defendant has made the decision to dismiss pending postconviction proceedings and discharge collateral counsel knowingly, freely, and voluntarily, the court shall enter an order dismissing all pending postconviction proceedings and discharging collateral counsel. But if the court determines that the defendant has not made the decision to dismiss pending postconviction proceedings and discharge collateral counsel knowingly, freely, and voluntarily, the court shall enter an order denying the motion without prejudice.

(8) If the court grants the motion:

(A) a copy of the motion, the order, and the transcript of the hearing or hearings conducted on the motion shall be forwarded to the Clerk of the Supreme Court of Florida within 30 days; and

(B) discharged counsel shall, within 10 days after issuance of the order, file with the clerk of the circuit court 2 copies of a notice seeking review in the Supreme Court of Florida, and shall, within 20 days after the filing of the transcript, serve an initial brief. Both the defendant and the state may serve responsive briefs. Briefs shall be served as prescribed by rule 9.210.

(9) If the court denies the motion, the defendant may seek review as prescribed by Florida Rule of Appellate Procedure 9.142(b).

(j) Attorney General Notification to Clerk. The Office of the Attorney General shall notify the clerk of the supreme court when it believes the defendant has completed his or her direct appeal, initial postconviction proceeding in state court, and habeas corpus proceeding and appeal therefrom in federal court. The Office of the Attorney General shall serve a copy of the notification on defendant's counsel of record.

Rule 3.853. Motion for Postconviction DNA Testing

(a) Purpose. This rule provides procedures for obtaining DNA (deoxyribonucleic acid) testing under sections 925.11 and 925.12, Florida Statutes.

(b) Contents of Motion. The motion for postconviction DNA testing must be under oath and must include the following:

(1) a statement of the facts relied upon in support of the motion, including a description of the physical evidence containing DNA to be tested and, if known, the present location or last known location of the evidence and how it originally was obtained;

(2) a statement that the evidence was not previously tested for DNA, or a statement that the results of previous DNA testing were inconclusive and that subsequent scientific developments in DNA testing techniques likely would produce a definitive result establishing that the movant is not the person who committed the crime;

(3) a statement that the movant is innocent and how the DNA testing requested by the motion will exonerate the movant of the crime for which the movant was sentenced, or a statement how the DNA testing will mitigate the sentence received by the movant for that crime;

(4) a statement that identification of the movant is a genuinely disputed issue in the case and why it is an issue or an explanation of how the DNA evidence would either exonerate the defendant or mitigate the sentence that the movant received;

(5) a statement of any other facts relevant to the motion; and

(6) a certificate that a copy of the motion has been served on the prosecuting authority.

(c) Procedure.

(1) Upon receipt of the motion, the clerk of the court shall file it and deliver the court file to the assigned judge.

(2) The court shall review the motion and deny it if it is facially insufficient. If the motion is facially sufficient, the prosecuting authority shall be ordered to respond to the motion within 30 days or such other time as may be ordered by the court.

(3) Upon receipt of the response of the prosecuting authority, the court shall review the response and enter an order on the merits of the motion or set the motion for hearing.

(4) In the event that the motion shall proceed to a hearing, the court may appoint counsel to assist the movant if the court determines that assistance of counsel is necessary and upon a determination of indigency pursuant to section 27.52, Florida Statutes.

(5) The court shall make the following findings when ruling on the motion:

(A) Whether it has been shown that physical evidence that may contain DNA still exists.

(B) Whether the results of DNA testing of that physical evidence likely would be admissible at trial and whether there exists reliable proof to establish that the evidence containing the tested DNA is authentic and would be admissible at a future hearing.

(C) Whether there is a reasonable probability that the movant would have been acquitted or would have received a lesser sentence if the DNA evidence had been admitted at trial.

(6) If the court orders DNA testing of the physical evidence, the cost of the testing may be assessed against the movant, unless the movant is indigent. If the movant is indigent, the state shall bear the cost of the DNA testing ordered by the court.

(7) The court-ordered DNA testing shall be ordered to be conducted by the Department of Law Enforcement or its designee, as provided by statute. However, the court, upon a showing of good cause, may order testing by another laboratory or agency certified by the American Society of Crime Laboratory Directors/Laboratory Accreditation Board (ASCLD/LAB) or Forensic Quality Services, Inc. (FQS) if requested by a movant who can bear the cost of such testing.

(8) The results of the DNA testing ordered by the court shall be provided in writing to the court, the movant, and the prosecuting authority.

(d) Time Limitations. The motion for postconviction DNA testing may be filed or considered at any time following the date that the judgment and sentence in the case becomes final.

(e) Rehearing. The movant may file a motion for rehearing of any order denying relief within 15 days after service of the order denying relief. The time for filing an appeal shall be tolled until an order on the motion for rehearing has been entered.

(f) Appeal. An appeal may be taken by any adversely affected party within 30 days from the date the order on the motion is rendered. All orders denying relief must include a statement that the movant has the right to appeal within 30 days after the order denying relief is rendered.

APPENDIX D – SELECTED RULES OF APPELLATE PROCEDURE

Rule 9.140. Appeal Proceedings in Criminal Cases

(a) Applicability. Appeal proceedings in criminal cases shall be as in civil cases except as modified by this rule.

(b) Appeals by Defendant.

(1) *Appeals Permitted.* A defendant may appeal

(A) a final judgment adjudicating guilt;

(B) a final order withholding adjudication after a finding of guilt;

(C) an order granting probation or community control, or both, whether or not guilt has been adjudicated;

(D) orders entered after final judgment or finding of guilt, including orders revoking or modifying probation or community control, or both, or orders denying relief under Florida Rule of Criminal Procedure 3.800(a), 3.801, 3.802, 3.850, 3.851, or 3.853;

(E) an unlawful or illegal sentence;

(F) a sentence, if the appeal is required or permitted by general law; or

(G) as otherwise provided by general law.

(2) Guilty or Nolo Contendere Pleas.

(A) Pleas. A defendant may not appeal from a guilty or nolo contendere plea except as follows:

(i) Reservation of Right to Appeal. A defendant who pleads guilty or nolo contendere may expressly reserve the right to appeal a prior dispositive order of the lower tribunal, identifying with particularity the point of law being reserved.

(ii) Appeals Otherwise Allowed. A defendant who pleads guilty or nolo contendere may otherwise directly appeal only

a. the lower tribunal's lack of subject matter jurisdiction;

b. a violation of the plea agreement, if preserved by a motion to withdraw plea;

c. an involuntary plea, if preserved by a motion to withdraw plea;

d. a sentencing error, if preserved; or

e. as otherwise provided by law.

(B) Record.

(i) Except for appeals under subdivision (b)(2)(A)(i) of this rule, the record for appeals involving a plea of guilty or nolo contendere shall be limited to:

a. all indictments, informations, affidavits of violation of probation or community control, and other charging documents;

b. the plea and sentencing hearing transcripts;

c. any written plea agreements;

d. any judgments, sentences, scoresheets, motions, and orders to correct or modify sentences, orders imposing, modifying, or revoking probation or community control, orders assessing costs, fees, fines, or restitution against the defendant, and any other documents relating to sentencing;

e. any motion to withdraw plea and order thereon;

f. notice of appeal, statement of judicial acts to be reviewed, directions to the clerk, and designation to the approved court reporter or approved transcriptionist.

(ii) Upon good cause shown, the court, or the lower tribunal before the record is electronically transmitted, may expand the record.

(3) *Commencement.* The defendant shall file the notice prescribed by rule 9.110(d) with the clerk of the lower tribunal at any time between rendition of a final judgment and 30 days following rendition of a written order imposing sentence. Copies shall be served on the state attorney and attorney general.

(4) *Cross-Appeal.* A defendant may cross-appeal by serving a notice within 10 days of service of the state's notice or service of an order on a motion pursuant to Florida Rule of Criminal Procedure 3.800(b)(2). Review of cross-appeals before trial is limited to related issues resolved in the same order being appealed.

(c) Appeals by the State.

(1) *Appeals Permitted.* The state may appeal an order

(A) dismissing an indictment or information or any count thereof or dismissing an affidavit charging the commission of a criminal offense, the violation of probation, the violation of community control, or the violation of any supervised correctional release;

(B) suppressing before trial confessions, admissions, or evidence obtained by search and seizure;
(C) granting a new trial;
(D) arresting judgment;
(E) granting a motion for judgment of acquittal after a jury verdict;
(F) discharging a defendant under Florida Rule of Criminal Procedure 3.191;
(G) discharging a prisoner on habeas corpus;
(H) finding a defendant incompetent or insane;
(I) finding a defendant intellectually disabled under Florida Rule of Criminal Procedure 3.203;
(J) granting relief under Florida Rule of Criminal Procedure 3.801, 3.850, 3.851, or 3.853;
(K) ruling on a question of law if a convicted defendant appeals the judgment of conviction;
(L) withholding adjudication of guilt in violation of general law;
(M) imposing an unlawful or illegal sentence or imposing a sentence outside the range permitted by the sentencing guidelines;
(N) imposing a sentence outside the range recommended by the sentencing guidelines;
(O) denying restitution; or
(P) as otherwise provided by general law for final orders.

(2) *Non-Final Orders.* The state as provided by general law may appeal to the circuit court non-final orders rendered in the county court.

(3) *Commencement.* The state shall file the notice prescribed by rule 9.110(d) with the clerk of the lower tribunal within 15 days of rendition of the order to be reviewed; provided that in an appeal by the state under rule 9.140(c)(1)(K), the state's notice of cross-appeal shall be filed within 10 days of service of defendant's notice or service of an order on a motion pursuant to Florida Rule of Criminal Procedure 3.800(b)(2). Copies shall be served on the defendant and the attorney of record. An appeal by the state shall stay further proceedings in the lower tribunal only by order of the lower tribunal.

(d) Withdrawal of Defense Counsel after Judgment and Sentence or after Appeal by State.

(1) The attorney of record for a defendant in a criminal proceeding shall not be relieved of any professional duties, or be permitted to withdraw as defense

counsel of record, except with approval of the lower tribunal on good cause shown on written motion, until either the time has expired for filing an authorized notice of appeal and no such notice has been filed by the defendant or the state, or after the following have been completed:

(A) a notice of appeal or cross-appeal has been filed on behalf of the defendant or the state;

(B) a statement of judicial acts to be reviewed has been filed if a transcript will require the expenditure of public funds;

(C) the defendant's directions to the clerk have been filed, if necessary;

(D) designations to the approved court reporter or approved transcriptionist have been filed for transcripts of those portions of the proceedings necessary to support the issues on appeal or, if transcripts will require the expenditure of public funds for the defendant, of those portions of the proceedings necessary to support the statement of judicial acts to be reviewed; and

(E) in publicly funded defense and state appeals, when the lower tribunal has entered an order appointing the office of the public defender for the local circuit, the district office of criminal conflict and civil regional counsel, or private counsel as provided by chapter 27, Florida Statutes, that office, or attorney shall remain counsel for the appeal until the record is electronically transmitted to the court. In publicly funded state appeals, defense counsel shall additionally file with the court a copy of the lower tribunal's order appointing the local public defender, the office of criminal conflict and civil regional counsel, or private counsel. In non-publicly funded defense and state appeals, retained appellate counsel shall file a notice of appearance in the court, or defense counsel of record shall file a motion to withdraw in the court, with service on the defendant, that states what the defendant's legal representation on appeal, if any, is expected to be. Documents filed in the court shall be served on the attorney general (or state attorney in appeals to the circuit court).

(2) Orders allowing withdrawal of counsel are conditional and counsel shall remain of record for the limited purpose of representing the defendant in the lower tribunal regarding any sentencing error the lower tribunal is authorized to address during the pendency of the direct appeal pursuant to Florida Rule of Criminal Procedure 3.800(b)(2).

(e) Sentencing Errors. A sentencing error may not be raised on appeal unless the alleged error has first been brought to the attention of the lower tribunal:

(1) at the time of sentencing; or

(2) by motion pursuant to Florida Rule of Criminal Procedure 3.800(b).

(f) Record.

(1) *Service.* The clerk of the lower tribunal shall prepare and serve the record prescribed by rule 9.200 within 50 days of the filing of the notice of appeal. However, the clerk shall not serve the record until all proceedings designated for transcription have been transcribed by the court reporter(s) and filed with the clerk. If the designated transcripts have not been filed by the date required for service of the record, the clerk shall file with the court, and serve on all parties and any court reporter whose transcript has not been filed, a notice of inability to complete the record, listing the transcripts not yet received. In cases where the transcripts are filed after a notice from the clerk, the clerk shall prepare and file the record within 20 days of receipt of the transcripts. An order granting an extension to the court reporter to transcribe designated proceedings shall toll the time for the clerk to serve this notice or the record on appeal.

(2) *Transcripts.*

(A) If a defendant's designation of a transcript of proceedings requires expenditure of public funds, trial counsel for the defendant (in conjunction with appellate counsel, if possible) shall serve, within 10 days of filing the notice, a statement of judicial acts to be reviewed, and a designation to the approved court reporter or approved transcriptionist requiring preparation of only so much of the proceedings as fairly supports the issue raised.

(B) Either party may file motions in the lower tribunal to reduce or expand the transcripts.

(C) Except as permitted in subdivision (f)(2)(D) of this rule, the parties shall designate the approved court reporter or approved transcriptionist to file with the clerk of the lower tribunal the transcripts for the court and sufficient paper copies for all parties exempt from service by e-mail as set forth in the Florida Rules of Judicial Administration.

(D) Non-indigent defendants represented by counsel may designate the approved court reporter or approved transcriptionist to prepare the transcripts. Counsel adopting this procedure shall, within 5 days of receipt of the transcripts from the approved court reporter or approved transcriptionist, file the transcripts. Counsel shall serve notice of the use of this procedure on the attorney general (or the state attorney in appeals to circuit court) and the clerk of the lower tribunal. Counsel shall attach a certificate to each transcript certifying that it is accurate and complete. When this procedure is used, the clerk of the lower tribunal upon conclusion of the appeal shall retain the transcript(s) for use as needed by the state in any collateral proceedings and shall not dispose of the transcripts without the consent of the Office of the Attorney General.

(E) In state appeals, the state shall designate the approved court reporter or approved transcriptionist to prepare and file with the clerk of the lower tribunal the transcripts and sufficient copies for all parties exempt from service by e-mail as set forth in the Florida Rules of Judicial Administration. Alternatively, the state may elect to use the procedure specified in subdivision (f)(2)(D) of this rule.

(F) The lower tribunal may by administrative order in publicly-funded cases direct the clerk of the lower tribunal rather than the approved court reporter or approved transcriptionist to prepare the necessary transcripts.

(3) *Retention of Documents.* Unless otherwise ordered by the court, the clerk of the lower tribunal shall retain any original documents.

(4) *Service of Copies.* The clerk of the lower tribunal shall serve copies of the record to the court, attorney general (or state attorney in appeals to circuit court), and all counsel appointed to represent indigent defendants on appeal. The clerk of the lower tribunal shall simultaneously serve copies of the index to all non-indigent defendants and, upon their request, copies of the record or portions thereof at the cost prescribed by law.

(5) *Return of Record.* Except in death penalty cases, the court shall return the record to the lower tribunal after final disposition of the appeal.

(6) *Supplemental Record for Motion to Correct Sentencing Error Pursuant to Florida Rule of Criminal Procedure 3.800(b)(2).*

(A) The clerk of circuit court shall automatically supplement the appellate record with any motion pursuant to Florida Rule of Criminal Procedure 3.800(b)(2), any response, any resulting order, and any amended sentence. The clerk shall electronically transmit the supplement to the court within 5 days of the filing of the order ruling on the motion. If an order is not filed within 60 days from the filing of the motion, this time shall run from the expiration of the 60-day period, and the clerk shall supplement the record with the motion and a statement that no order was timely filed.

(B) If any appellate counsel determines that a transcript of a proceeding relating to such a motion is required to review the sentencing issue, appellate counsel shall, within 5 days from the transmittal of the supplement described in subdivision (A), designate those portions of the proceedings not on file deemed necessary for transcription and inclusion in the record. A copy of the designation shall be filed with the court. The procedure for this supplementation shall be in accordance with this subdivision, except that counsel is not required to file a revised statement of judicial acts to be reviewed, the approved court reporter or approved transcriptionist shall deliver the transcript within 15 days, and the clerk shall supplement the record with the transcript within 5 days of its receipt.

(g) Briefs.

(1) *Briefs on the merits.* Initial briefs shall be served within 30 days of service of the record or designation of appointed counsel, whichever is later. Additional briefs shall be served as prescribed by rule 9.210.

(2) *Anders Briefs.*

(A) If appointed counsel files a brief stating that an appeal would be frivolous, the court shall independently review the record to discover any arguable issues apparent on the face of the record. Upon the discovery of an arguable issue, other than an unpreserved sentencing, disposition, or commitment order error, the court shall order briefing on the issues identified by the court.

(B) Upon discovery of an unpreserved sentencing, disposition, or commitment order error, the court may strike the brief and allow for a motion pursuant to Florida Rule of Criminal Procedure 3.800(b)(2) or Florida Rule of Juvenile Procedure 8.135(b)(2) to be filed. The court's order may contain deadlines for the cause to be resolved within a reasonable time.

(h) Post-Trial Release.

(1) *Appeal by Defendant.* The lower tribunal may hear a motion for post-trial release pending appeal before or after a notice is filed; provided that the defendant may not be released from custody until the notice is filed.

(2) *Appeal by State.* An incarcerated defendant charged with a bailable offense shall on motion be released on the defendant's own recognizance pending an appeal by the state, unless the lower tribunal for good cause stated in an order determines otherwise.

(3) *Denial of Post-Trial Release.* All orders denying post-trial release shall set forth the factual basis on which the decision was made and the reasons therefor.

(4) *Review.* Review of an order relating to post-trial release shall be by the court on motion.

(i) Scope of Review. The court shall review all rulings and orders appearing in the record necessary to pass upon the grounds of an appeal. In the interest of justice, the court may grant any relief to which any party is entitled.

Rule 9.141. Review Proceedings in Collateral or Post-Conviction Criminal Cases

(a) Death Penalty Cases. This rule does not apply to death penalty cases.

(b) Appeals from Post-Conviction Proceedings Under Florida Rule of Criminal Procedure 3.800(a), 3.801, 3.850, or 3.853.

(1) *Applicability of Civil Appellate Procedures.* Appeal proceedings under this subdivision shall be as in civil cases, except as modified by this rule.

(2) *Summary Grant or Denial of All Claims Raised in a Motion Without Evidentiary Hearing.*

(A) Record. When a motion for post-conviction relief under rule 3.800(a), 3.801, 3.850, or 3.853 is granted or denied without an evidentiary hearing, the clerk of the lower tribunal shall electronically transmit to the court, as the record, the motion, response, reply, order on the motion, motion for rehearing, response, reply, order on the motion for rehearing, and attachments to any of the foregoing, together with the certified copy of the notice of appeal.

(B) Index. Unless directed otherwise by the court, the clerk of the lower tribunal shall not index or paginate the record or send copies of the index or record to the parties.

(C) Briefs or Responses.

(i) Briefs are not required, but the appellant may serve an initial brief within 30 days of filing the notice of appeal. The appellee need not file an answer brief unless directed by the court. The appellant may serve a reply brief as prescribed by rule 9.210.

(ii) The court may request a response from the appellee before ruling, regardless of whether the appellant filed an initial brief. The appellant may serve a reply within 20 days after service of the response. The response and reply shall not exceed the page limits set forth in rule 9.210 for answer briefs and reply briefs.

(D) Disposition. On appeal from the denial of relief, unless the record shows conclusively that the appellant is entitled to no relief, the order shall be reversed and the cause remanded for an evidentiary hearing or other appropriate relief.

(3) *Grant or Denial of Motion after an Evidentiary Hearing was Held on One or More Claims.*

(A) Transcription. In the absence of designations to the court reporter, the notice of appeal filed by an indigent pro se litigant in a rule 3.801, 3.850, or 3.853 appeal after an evidentiary hearing shall serve as the designation to the court reporter for the transcript of the evidentiary hearing. Within 5 days of receipt of the notice of appeal, the clerk of the lower tribunal shall request the appropriate court reporter to transcribe the evidentiary hearing and shall send the court reporter a copy of the notice, the date of the hearing to be transcribed, the name of the judge, and a copy of this rule.

(B) Record.

(i) When a motion for post-conviction relief under rule 3.801, 3.850, or 3.853 is granted or denied after an evidentiary hearing, the clerk of the lower tribunal shall index, paginate, and electronically transmit to the court as the record, within 50 days of the filing of the notice of appeal, the notice of appeal, motion, response, reply, order on the motion, motion for rehearing, response, reply, order on the motion for rehearing, and attachments to any of the foregoing, as well as the transcript of the evidentiary hearing.

(ii) Appellant may direct the clerk to include in the record any other documents that were before the lower tribunal at the hearing. If the clerk is directed to include in the record a previously prepared appellate record involving the appellant, the clerk need not reindex or repaginate it.

(iii) The clerk of the lower tribunal shall serve copies of the record on the attorney general (or state attorney in appeals to the circuit court), all counsel appointed to represent indigent defendants on appeal, and any pro se indigent defendant. The clerk of the lower tribunal shall simultaneously serve copies of the index on all nonindigent defendants and, at their request, copies of the record or portions of it at the cost prescribed by law.

(C) Briefs. Initial briefs shall be served within 30 days of service of the record or its index. Additional briefs shall be served as prescribed by rule 9.210.

(c) Petitions Seeking Belated Appeal or Belated Discretionary Review.

(1) *Applicability*. This subdivision governs petitions seeking belated appeals or belated discretionary review.

(2) *Treatment as Original Proceedings*. Review proceedings under this subdivision shall be treated as original proceedings under rule 9.100, except as modified by this rule.

(3) *Forum*. Petitions seeking belated review shall be filed in the court to which the appeal or discretionary review should have been taken.

(4) *Contents*. The petition shall be in the form prescribed by rule 9.100, may include supporting documents, and shall recite in the statement of facts.

(A) the date and nature of the lower tribunal's order sought to be reviewed;

(B) the name of the lower tribunal rendering the order;

(C) the nature, disposition, and dates of all previous court proceedings;

(D) if a previous petition was filed, the reason the claim in the present petition was not raised previously;

(E) the nature of the relief sought; and

(F) the specific acts sworn to by the petitioner or petitioner's counsel that constitute the basis for entitlement to belated appeal or belated discretionary review, as outlined below:

(i) A petition seeking belated appeal must state whether the petitioner requested counsel to proceed with the appeal and the date of any such request, or if the petitioner was misadvised as to the availability of appellate review or the status of filing a notice of appeal. A petition seeking belated discretionary review must state whether counsel advised the petitioner of the results of the appeal and the date of any such notification, or if counsel misadvised the petitioner as to the opportunity for seeking discretionary review, or

(ii) A petition seeking belated appeal or belated discretionary review must identify the circumstances unrelated to counsel's action or inaction, including names of individuals involved and date(s) of the occurrence(s), that were beyond the petitioner's control and otherwise interfered with the petitioner's ability to file a timely appeal or notice to invoke, as applicable.

(5) *Time Limits.*

(A) A petition for belated appeal shall not be filed more than 2 years after the expiration of time for filing the notice of appeal from a final order, unless it alleges under oath with a specific factual basis that the petitioner was unaware a notice of appeal had not been timely filed or was not advised of the right to an appeal or was otherwise prevented from timely filing the notice of appeal due to circumstances beyond the petitioner's control, and could not have ascertained such facts by the exercise of reasonable diligence. In no case shall a petition for belated appeal be filed more than 4 years after the expiration of time for filing the notice of appeal.

(B) A petition for belated discretionary review shall not be filed more than 2 years after the expiration of time for filing the notice to invoke discretionary review from a final order, unless it alleges under oath with a specific factual basis that the petitioner was unaware such notice had not been timely filed or was not advised of the results of the appeal, or was otherwise prevented from timely filing the notice due to circumstances beyond the petitioner's control, and that the petitioner could not have ascertained such facts by the exercise of reasonable diligence. In no case shall a petition for belated discretionary review be filed more than 4 years after the expiration of time for filing the notice to invoke discretionary review from a final order.

(6) *Procedure.*

(A) The petitioner shall serve a copy of a petition for belated appeal on the attorney general and state attorney. The petitioner shall serve a copy of a petition for belated discretionary review on the attorney general.

(B) The court may by order identify any provision of this rule that the petition fails to satisfy and, pursuant to rule 9.040(d), allow the petitioner a specified time to serve an amended petition.

(C) The court may dismiss a second or successive petition if it does not allege new grounds and the prior determination was on the merits, or if a failure to assert the grounds was an abuse of procedure.

(D) An order granting a petition for belated appeal shall be filed with the lower tribunal and treated as the notice of appeal, if no previous notice has been filed. An order granting a petition for belated discretionary review or belated appeal of a decision of a district court of appeal shall be filed with the district court and treated as a notice to invoke discretionary jurisdiction or notice of appeal, if no previous notice has been filed.

(d) Petitions Alleging Ineffective Assistance of Appellate Counsel.

(1) *Applicability.* This subdivision governs petitions alleging ineffective assistance of appellate counsel.

(2) *Treatment as Original Proceedings.* Review proceedings under this subdivision shall be treated as original proceedings under rule 9.100, except as modified by this rule.

(3) *Forum.* Petitions alleging ineffective assistance of appellate counsel shall be filed in the court to which the appeal was taken.

(4) *Contents.* The petition shall be in the form prescribed by rule 9.100, may include supporting documents, and shall recite in the statement of facts:

(A) the date and nature of the lower tribunal's order subject to the disputed appeal;

(B) the name of the lower tribunal rendering the order;

(C) the nature, disposition, and dates of all previous court proceedings;

(D) if a previous petition was filed, the reason the claim in the present petition was not raised previously;

(E) the nature of the relief sought; and

(F) the specific acts sworn to by the petitioner or petitioner's counsel that constitute the alleged ineffective assistance of counsel.

(5) *Time Limits.* A petition alleging ineffective assistance of appellate counsel on direct review shall not be filed more than 2 years after the judgment and sentence become final on direct review unless it alleges under oath with a specific factual basis that the petitioner was affirmatively misled about the

results of the appeal by counsel. In no case shall a petition alleging ineffective assistance of appellate counsel on direct review be filed more than 4 years after the judgment and sentence become final on direct review.

(6) *Procedure.*

(A) The petitioner shall serve a copy of the petition on the attorney general.

(B) The court may by order identify any provision of this rule that the petition fails to satisfy and, pursuant to rule 9.040(d), allow the petitioner a specified time to serve an amended petition.

(C) The court may dismiss a second or successive petition if it does not allege new grounds and the prior determination was on the merits, or if a failure to assert the grounds was an abuse of procedure.

Rule 9.210. Briefs

(a) Generally. In addition to briefs on jurisdiction under rule 9.120(d), the only briefs permitted to be filed by the parties in any one proceeding are the initial brief, the answer brief, a reply brief, and a cross-reply brief. All briefs required by these rules shall be prepared as follows:

(1) When not filed in electronic format, briefs shall be printed, typewritten, or duplicated on opaque, white, unglossed paper. The dimensions of each page of a brief, regardless of format, shall be 8 ½ by 11 inches.

(2) The lettering in briefs shall be black and in distinct type, double-spaced, with margins no less than 1 inch. Lettering in script or type made in imitation of handwriting shall not be permitted. Footnotes and quotations may be single spaced and shall be in the same size type, with the same spacing between characters, as the text in the body of the brief. Headings and subheadings shall be at least as large as the brief's text and may be single-spaced. Computer-generated briefs shall be filed in either Times New Roman 14-point font or Courier New 12-point font. All computer-generated briefs shall contain a certificate of compliance signed by counsel, or the party if unrepresented, certifying that the brief complies with the font requirements of this rule. The certificate of compliance shall be contained in the brief immediately following the certificate of service.

(3) Briefs filed in paper format shall not be stapled or bound.

(4) The cover sheet of each brief shall state the name of the court, the style of the cause, including the case number if assigned, the lower tribunal, the party on whose behalf the brief is filed, the type of brief, and the name and address of the attorney filing the brief.

(5) The page limits for briefs shall be as follows:

(A) Briefs on jurisdiction shall not exceed 10 pages.

(B) Except as provided in subdivisions (a)(5)(C) and (a)(5)(D) of this rule, the initial and answer briefs shall not exceed 50 pages and the reply brief shall not exceed 15 pages. If a cross-appeal is filed, the appellee's answer/cross-initial brief shall not exceed 85 pages, and the appellant's reply/cross-answer brief shall not exceed 50 pages, not more than 15 of which shall be devoted to argument replying to the answer portion of the appellee's answer/cross-initial brief. Cross-reply briefs shall not exceed 15 pages.

(C) In an appeal from a judgment of conviction imposing a sentence of death or from an order ruling after an evidentiary hearing on an initial postconviction motion filed under Florida Rule of Criminal Procedure 3.851, the initial and answer briefs shall not exceed 100 pages and the reply brief shall not exceed 35 pages. If a cross-appeal is filed, the appellee's answer/cross-initial brief shall not exceed 150 pages, and the appellant's reply/cross-answer brief shall not exceed 100 pages, not more than 35 of which shall be devoted to argument replying to the answer portion of the appellee's answer/cross-initial brief. Cross-reply briefs shall not exceed 35 pages.

(D) In an appeal from an order summarily denying an initial postconviction motion filed under Florida Rule of Criminal Procedure 3.851, a ruling on a successive postconviction motion filed under Florida Rule of Criminal Procedure 3.851, a finding that a defendant is intellectually disabled as a bar to execution under Florida Rule of Criminal Procedure 3.203, or a ruling on a motion for postconviction DNA testing filed under Florida Rule of Criminal Procedure 3.853, the initial and answer briefs shall not exceed 75 pages. Reply briefs shall not exceed 25 pages.

(E) The cover sheet, the tables of contents and citations, the certificates of service and compliance, and the signature block for the brief's author shall be excluded from the page limits in subdivisions (a)(5)(A)-(a)(5)(D). All pages not excluded from the computation shall be consecutively numbered. The court may permit longer briefs.

(b) Contents of Initial Brief. The initial brief shall contain the following, in order:

(1) A table of contents listing the sections of the brief, including headings and subheadings that identify the issues presented for review, with references to the pages on which each appears.

(2) A table of citations with cases listed alphabetically, statutes and other authorities, and the pages of the brief on which each citation appears. See rule 9.800 for a uniform citation system.

(3) A statement of the case and of the facts, which shall include the nature of the case, the course of the proceedings, and the disposition in the lower tribunal. References to the appropriate pages of the record or transcript shall be made.

(4) A summary of argument, suitably paragraphed, condensing succinctly, accurately, and clearly the argument actually made in the body of the brief. It should not be a mere repetition of the headings under which the argument is arranged. It should seldom exceed 2 and never 5 pages.

(5) Argument with regard to each issue, with citation to appropriate authorities, and including the applicable appellate standard of review.

(6) A conclusion, of not more than 1 page, setting forth the precise relief sought.

(7) A certificate of service.

(8) A certificate of compliance for computer-generated briefs.

(c) Contents of Answer Brief. The answer brief shall be prepared in the same manner as the initial brief, provided that the statement of the case and of the facts may be omitted, if the corresponding section of the initial brief is deemed satisfactory. If a cross-appeal has been filed, the answer brief shall include the issues in the cross-appeal that are presented for review, and argument in support of those issues.

(d) Contents of Reply Brief. The reply brief shall contain argument in response and rebuttal to argument presented in the answer brief. A table of contents, a table of citations, a certificate of service, and, for computer-generated briefs, a certificate of compliance shall be included in the same manner as in the initial brief.

(e) Contents of Cross-Reply Brief. The cross-reply brief is limited to rebuttal of argument of the cross-appellee. A table of contents, a table of citations, a certificate of service, and, for computer-generated briefs, a certificate of compliance shall be included in the same manner as in the initial brief.

(f) Times for Service of Briefs. The times for serving jurisdiction and initial briefs are prescribed by rules 9.110, 9.120, 9.130, and 9.140. Unless otherwise required, the answer brief shall be served within 20 days after service of the initial brief; the reply brief, if any, shall be served within 20 days after service of the answer brief; and the cross-reply brief, if any, shall be served within 20 days thereafter.

(g) Citations. Counsel are requested to use the uniform citation system prescribed by rule 9.800.

APPENDIX E – JURISDICTION OF FLORIDA COURTS

ARTICLE V, FLORIDA CONSTITUTION

SECTION 3. **Supreme court.**

(a) ORGANIZATION. The supreme court shall consist of seven justices. Of the seven justices, each appellate district shall have at least one justice elected or appointed from the district to the supreme court who is a resident of the district at the time of the original appointment or election. Five justices shall constitute a quorum. The concurrence of four justices shall be necessary to a decision. When recusals for cause would prohibit the court from convening because of the requirements of this section, judges assigned to temporary duty may be substituted for justices.

(b) JURISDICTION. The supreme court:

(1) Shall hear appeals from final judgments of trial courts imposing the death penalty and from decisions of district courts of appeal declaring invalid a state statute or a provision of the state constitution.

(2) When provided by general law, shall hear appeals from final judgments entered in proceedings for the validation of bonds or certificates of indebtedness and shall review action of statewide agencies relating to rates or service of utilities providing electric, gas, or telephone service.

(3) May review any decision of a district court of appeal that expressly declares valid a state statute, or that expressly construes a provision of the state or federal constitution, or that expressly affects a class of constitutional or state officers, or that expressly and directly conflicts with a decision of another district court of appeal or of the supreme court on the same question of law.

(4) May review any decision of a district court of appeal that passes upon a question certified by it to be of great public importance, or that is certified by it to be in direct conflict with a decision of another district court of appeal.

(5) May review any order or judgment of a trial court certified by the district court of appeal in which an appeal is pending to be of great public importance, or to have a great effect on the proper administration of justice throughout the state, and certified to require immediate resolution by the supreme court.

(6) May review a question of law certified by the Supreme Court of the United States or a United States Court of Appeals which is determinative of the cause and for which there is no controlling precedent of the supreme court of Florida.

(7) May issue writs of prohibition to courts and all writs necessary to the complete exercise of its jurisdiction.

(8) May issue writs of mandamus and *quo warranto* to state officers and state agencies.

(9) May, or any justice may, issue writs of habeas corpus returnable before the supreme court or any justice, a district court of appeal or any judge thereof, or any circuit judge.
(10) Shall, when requested by the attorney general pursuant to the provisions of Section 10 of Article IV, render an advisory opinion of the justices, addressing issues as provided by general law.

(c) CLERK AND MARSHAL. The supreme court shall appoint a clerk and a marshal who shall hold office during the pleasure of the court and perform such duties as the court directs. Their compensation shall be fixed by general law. The marshal shall have the power to execute the process of the court throughout the state, and in any county may deputize the sheriff or a deputy sheriff for such purpose.

SECTION 4. **District courts of appeal.**

(a) ORGANIZATION. There shall be a district court of appeal serving each appellate district. Each district court of appeal shall consist of at least three judges. Three judges shall consider each case and the concurrence of two shall be necessary to a decision.

(b) JURISDICTION.
(1) District courts of appeal shall have jurisdiction to hear appeals, that may be taken as a matter of right, from final judgments or orders of trial courts, including those entered on review of administrative action, not directly appealable to the supreme court or a circuit court. They may review interlocutory orders in such cases to the extent provided by rules adopted by the supreme court.
(2) District courts of appeal shall have the power of direct review of administrative action, as prescribed by general law.
(3) A district court of appeal or any judge thereof may issue writs of habeas corpus returnable before the court or any judge thereof or before any circuit judge within the territorial jurisdiction of the court. A district court of appeal may issue writs of mandamus, certiorari, prohibition, quo warranto, and other writs necessary to the complete exercise of its jurisdiction. To the extent necessary to dispose of all issues in a cause properly before it, a district court of appeal may exercise any of the appellate jurisdiction of the circuit courts.

(c) CLERKS AND MARSHALS. Each district court of appeal shall appoint a clerk and a marshal who shall hold office during the pleasure of the court and perform such duties as the court directs. Their compensation shall be fixed by general law. The marshal shall have the power to execute the process of the court throughout the territorial jurisdiction of the court, and in any county may deputize the sheriff or a deputy sheriff for such purpose.

SECTION 5. **Circuit courts.**

(a) ORGANIZATION. There shall be a circuit court serving each judicial circuit.

(b) JURISDICTION. The circuit courts shall have original jurisdiction not vested in the county courts, and jurisdiction of appeals when provided by general law. They shall have the power to issue writs of mandamus, quo warranto, certiorari, prohibition and habeas corpus, and all writs necessary or proper to the complete exercise of their jurisdiction. Jurisdiction of the circuit court shall be uniform throughout the state. They shall have the power of direct review of administrative action prescribed by general law.

SECTION 6. **County courts.**

(a) ORGANIZATION. There shall be a county court in each county. There shall be one or more judges for each county court as prescribed by general law.

(b) JURISDICTION. The county courts shall exercise the jurisdiction prescribed by general law. Such jurisdiction shall be uniform throughout the state.

ABOUT THE AUTHOR

Loren D. Rhoton is an attorney in private practice in Tampa, Florida. Mr. Rhoton graduated from the University of Toledo College of Law and has been a member in good standing with The Florida Bar since his admission to practice in 1995. Mr. Rhoton's office specializes in criminal appeal/postconviction cases.

Mr. Rhoton is a member of The Florida Bar's Appellate Practice Division. He is also a member of the U.S. District Court, in and for the Southern, Middle and Northern Districts of Florida. Mr. Rhoton is licensed to practice before the U.S. Court of Appeals for the 11th Circuit and is also certified to practice before the U.S. Supreme Court. Mr. Rhoton regularly practices before Federal District Courts and the U.S. Court of Appeals for the 11th Circuit.

Mr. Rhoton typically deals with clients who have lengthy prison sentences. He has investigated and pursued thousands of postconviction cases. He has practiced in all phases of the Florida Judicial System, all the way from misdemeanor county courts up to the Florida Supreme Court. Additionally, Mr. Rhoton has been directly responsible for amendments to Florida Rule of Criminal Procedure 3.850 (the main vehicle for most postconviction actions). Mr. Rhoton was appointed by the Florida Supreme Court to the Florida Criminal Rules Steering Committee, Subcommittee on Postconviction Relief, which focused on rewriting Florida Rule of Criminal Procedure 3.850. Mr. Rhoton worked on said subcommittee with judges and other governmental officials in an effort to improve the administration and execution of postconviction proceedings. Mr. Rhoton's role on the committee was to advocate for changes that were beneficial to postconviction litigants.

For over a decade, Mr. Rhoton authored a bimonthly article, *Post Conviction Corner*, for Florida Prison Legal Perspectives. Thereafter he commenced publication of his own postconviction newsletter, The Florida Postconviction Journal. Selected articles from *Post Conviction Corner* and the Florida Postconviction Journal have been compiled and printed in a legal self-help book, *Postconviction Relief for the Florida Prisoner*. Mr. Rhoton previously served on the Board of Directors of the Florida Prisoners' Legal Aid Organization and the Florida Postconviction Legal Aid Organization, Inc.

Contact Loren Rhoton at:
412 E. Madison Street
Suite 1111
Tampa, Florida 33602
Phone: 813-226-3138
Email: lorenrhoton@rhotonpostconviciton.com
Website: www.rhotonpostconviction.com

www.ingramcontent.com/pod-product-compliance
Lightning Source LLC
LaVergne TN
LVHW082345200926
848481LV00012B/3458
* 9 7 8 0 9 8 2 2 8 0 0 8 9 *